If you are tired of books on marriage that do nothing but make you feel guilty and cause you to wonder if the author was living on another planet, you are going to love James Price's book, *The Marriage Guarantee*. It's a practical, honest, profound, and Biblical book on what may be the most important issue of our time. Read this book and give it to your friends. You will "rise up and call me blessed" for having recommended it to you.

DR. STEVE BROWN, AUTHOR, RADIO BROADCASTER, AND
SEMINARY PROFESSOR
BIBLE TEACHER, KEY LIFE NETWORK

Through this very personal journey of family life and friendships, James Price gives us all valuable insights for happier and holier relationships.

DR. JOEL C. HUNTER, AUTHOR
SENIOR PASTOR, NORTHLAND, A CHURCH DISTRIBUTED
AUTHOR, *INNERSTATE 80* & *A NEW KIND OF CONSERVATIVE*

the MARRIAGE GUARANTEE

Promises You Can Count On!

JAMES PRICE

PRACTICAL ADVICE FROM THE AUTHOR OF MARRIAGE

M*the*ARRIAGE GUARANTEE

Promises You Can Count On!

Oviedo, Florida

The Marriage Guarantee—Promises You Can Count On!
by James Price

Published by HigherLife Development Services, Inc.
400 Fontana Circle
Building 1 – Suite 105
Oviedo, Florida 32765
(407) 563-4806
www.ahigherlife.com

Unless otherwise noted, scripture quotations are from *The Holy Bible: New International Version* ®. Copyright © 1973, 1978, 1984 by International Bible Society. Used by permission of Zondervan Publishing House. All rights reserved.

Scripture quotations noted KJV are from *The Holy Bible: King James Version*. Cambridge, 1769. Used by permission. All rights reserved.

Scripture quotations noted NKJV are from *The New King James Version*. Copyright © 1979, 1980, 1982, 1990, 1994 by Thomas Nelson, Inc. Used by permission. All rights reserved.

DEDICATION

To my wife, Cindy Price, I love you more every day.

TABLE OF CONTENTS

ACKNOWLEDGMENTS

To my wife, Cindy, who continues to fascinate me and who was always willing to have another fight so I could have more material for my book. (It was a running joke for the past year and a half.) I love it when you laugh at yourself—you are amazing!

To my children Rosa, Kelly, Matt, and Heather—I pray that God can use this book to help you be the best husbands and wives you can be and that you would never forget the purpose of marriage.

To the future spouses of my children—I have prayed for you since my children were little. I have prayed specifically that God would keep you safe and would show Himself to you and prepare you to have wonderful, godly marriages. I cannot wait to meet you!

To my parents for praying for my wife for so many years before I met her and for setting such a great example of what a godly marriage is all about.

In memory of my father-in-law and to my mother-in-law for doing such a great job raising my wife and keeping her safe.

To our pastor, Dr. Joel Hunter, and all of the staff at Northland, A Church Distributed, for working so hard to serve our congregation and for the input you have had in our lives.

To all of the young couples that we have worked with over the years in pre-married class, it truly has been a privilege to be invited into your lives. Thank you for keeping us young and don't forget to call home occasionally.

A special thanks to Evrod, Rusty, Devvone and others who allowed me to use their words to illustrate sections of the book.

And finally, to all of our friends who have provided good sounding boards for the topics of the book.

We love you all and hope to see many years of fun and fellowship.

INTRODUCTION

YOU ARE ABOUT to read a very personal love story about my marriage, so I want to introduce myself and my lovely wife and give you a little background on us that I think will help as you begin to read our story.

I grew up with my two brothers, Jeff and Joel, in Venezuela, South America, where our parents, Joe and Jana Price, were missionaries to a primitive tribal group. They spent over forty years translating the Bible in the native language and taught the Panare Indians to read and write their own language while teaching them God's word.

I met my wife, Cindy, in Florida at Northland, A Church Distributed, while in leadership of the single group ministry.

About six months after meeting Cindy, I led a short term mission trip to Venezuela with fifteen singles from church, including Cindy. On the last leg of our trip, we all rode in the back of a cattle truck, and as we neared the valley where my childhood home was, I said to her "You know, there are diamonds in those hills." Although it was a true statement, she did not get the hint of things to come.

After work one day, I took her to the waterfalls at the front of the valley where I spent a lot of time as a young boy. We traveled to the falls in our old jeep. All we had was our swim suits, a raft, and some goggles. We hiked up the mountain a ways and arrived at a crystal clear basin at the base of the falls and began a refreshing swim. I waited just long enough to avoid suspicion, and then I said, "They really have found diamonds in these mountains. Let's go diving for diamonds."

Still, she did not seem to know what was about to happen. I handed her the goggles, grabbed her hand, and led her a few yards away where I had carefully hidden a diamond ring upon our arrival. I wedged the ring in the end of a stick and buried the stick upright in the sand so the diamond could be easily seen. When she saw the glimmer in the sand and then saw the gold attached, she grabbed the ring and the stick it was attached to and surfaced with great excitement.

After she calmed down and caught her breath, I asked her to marry me. Of course, she said, "Yes!"

We took a few pictures holding the camera at arm's length, and then she asked, "What about my parents?" I told her I had asked for her mother's blessing before leaving the home. And then she said, "What about my Dad?" I had not met her Dad yet. He lived in Hawaii at the time and I had heard of his sense of humor. Shortly after we started dating, Cindy had sent him a picture of me with about ten alligators (Cayman) that I had killed last time I visited home and a note saying, "This is the guy I am dating."

So in response to her question, I said "He will receive the frozen alligator head in the mail today." I told her of the note that accompanied the unusual package. It said, "I know that Cindy sent you a picture of me and some alligators and that she told you about the Panare Indian custom—how a man in the tribe will present animals he has killed to the father of the woman he wants to marry to show that he can provide for her. What she did not tell you was that the head of an animal is the most precious and desired part of the animal, and I want you to know that your daughter is very precious to me. And with that, I ask for your blessing on our marriage. I will be asking her to marry me while on our trip to Venezuela."

And that is how this love story begins.

Chapter 1

MARRIAGE DEGREE

WHY AREN'T WE required to have a marriage degree before getting married? We have to study, take tests, and "make the grade" for everything else in life. Think about it—we study for years and often go into debt just to get the right job. In most cases, we still cannot go right into our profession. We have to study more and take more tests to get the license or certification required to get the job. For example, my wife is a financial planner, and she had to study hard for years and get several certifications before becoming a CFP (Certified Financial Planner). She sacrificed a lot to get that designation; I saw all the studying she had to do. And that is still not enough! She is required to complete continuing education courses every year to keep the designation.

And what if you want to be an attorney or a doctor? You will have to study for years and get a degree and license to practice, and, even then, that won't necessarily make you a good doctor or attorney. We even have to study and take a test with a passing grade to be able to get a license to drive. You've probably noticed as you drive to work every morning that these tests are not difficult enough and allow some people behind the wheel who definitely should not be driving. My point is that we work very hard and study sometimes for years to get the job we want and even that is not a guarantee that we will get the job and be able to keep it. Why aren't we required to do the same before we get married? After all, it is one of the most complex relationships on earth. We have to perform surgery on our hearts all the time. Even if we have studied the manual, our chances of success are limited. It is only with continuing education and regular conversations with the professor that we can have any success at all. And when it comes to performing surgery on our spouses' hearts, that is not a job we can handle. Show me a man who understands a woman's heart. Most will say it's impossible. And show me a woman who has figured out how to tame a man's heart, and I will tell you she has done the wrong thing. He is supposed to be wild—it's what makes him a man. So why shouldn't we be required to get a degree before getting married? All you have to do is walk into the court house and say "I do"—no other requirements. Some will seek pre-married counseling as a choice. I have had the privilege of helping couples get ready for marriage, but even three or four sessions of counseling before getting married just isn't enough.

Most new couples will say, "You don't understand. We are different—we understand each other and we're in love." And, after being married sometimes only weeks, later they say, "You were right about…" Fill in the blank with any number of issues. They have often said to me, "We thought we would not face the issues you discussed, but we were wrong." It bothers me when I suggest a book about marriage and people don't take the time to read it. By far the most relevant book about marriage is none other than the Bible. You see, marriage was instituted by God—this is a line I often use when performing a marriage ceremony. If God designed it, then He must know a little about it. So we need to be studying His Word to help us become better at being married. It's never too late. Whether you are getting married or have been married for years, you need to study how to be better at it and study God's example on how to love your spouse better.

> Study to shew thyself approved unto God, a workman that needeth not to be ashamed, rightly dividing the word of truth. (2 Tim. 2:15 KJV)

We have to study and prepare for life and marriage. And we have to commit the vows of the scriptures to memory so that we may be able to fight the battle. The battle is against what the world says about marriage. Prepare yourself for this battle:

> I have hidden your word in my heart that I might not sin against you. (Ps. 119:11)

> Therefore put on the full armor of God, so that when the day of evil comes, you may be able to stand your ground, and after you have done everything, to stand. (Eph. 6:13)

Putting on the armor and fighting the battle is just another way of saying READ what God says in His Word, know Him better, pursue Christ likeness, arm yourself with the sword of truth, memorize God's Word, and take it with you.

The sword of truth was the foundational topic of my son's thirteenth birthday celebration. In an earlier year, when my niece turned thirteen, my brother performed a little ceremony where he spoke to his daughter about foundational topics and in the end asked her to wear a promise ring, agreeing publicly to dedicate her life to God and commit to purity. When my son approached thirteen, I wanted to have the opportunity to do the same sort of thing but did not think a ring would communicate the message very well for a young man. I had heard of fathers doing a rite-of-passage ceremony and liked the little I heard. So I decided that I would buy my son a sword and ask him to hang it on his wall to remind him of the commitments he had made. We set a date and gathered with friends and family at our home. I began the ceremony by having my son sit in a chair across from me while I spoke to him about the Word of God as his instruction book for life. I encouraged him to use his own words for good and emphasized how important it is to choose his words carefully when speaking to his parents, his sister, and his friends. I stressed the importance of memorizing the scriptures. I told him the story of the two bulldogs.

Imagine you had two bulldogs—one white and one black—that were in separate pens. The white one represents all that is good and godly. The black one represents all the world has to offer. Now, what if you went out every day and only fed the black one but neglected the white one. Which one would be stronger? Of course my son answered that the one you feed the most is going to be the stronger one. I went on to say that feeding the dogs represents what you do every day. What you see, what you hear, and what you do. The moral of the story is that if you spend too much time welcoming the input of the world and not enough time reading God's Word, listening to godly people, and doing what you know is right, then you will be feeding the wrong dog.

The problem with this story is that someone is always feeding the black dog; there is so much food for him. If we are going to catch up, we really need to work at it.

If we are not reading scripture and memorizing what it says, then we are fighting a losing battle or, as I often like to say, we need to put up mental road blocks.

Mental road blocks are anything that allows us to not "go there." If you are married, you have probably even heard these words from your spouse: "Don't go there..." On those occasions when your spouse has just said something hurtful, you may want to respond to him or her in a way that is not honoring to God. Our natural reaction in such circumstances is to respond with something like this: "But you always..." or "You never..." A good road block for this would be:

> Do not let any unwholesome talk come out of your mouths, but only what is helpful for building others up according to their needs, that it may benefit those who listen. (Eph. 4:29)

Words are the foundation. God's Word is alive and cannot be matched. Reading His Word is by far the best thing we can ever do. It also helps to read books that direct us to the scriptures necessary to build the road blocks. Feed the white bulldog! Read God's love letter to you. Study, hide it in your heart, put on the armor, and fight for what is right before God.

So the next time you pick up the Holy Bible, think to your-self, *I am going to study to be the best husband or wife I can possibly be.* Even better, pick it up together with that purpose in mind, and pray together that God would teach you.

READ! It just may save your marriage.

Chapter 2

THE PURPOSE OF MARRIAGE

WHAT IS THE purpose of marriage? For every person you ask you will probably get a different answer. But if God truly instituted marriage (and He did), then God has to be a key factor in defining the purpose of marriage. So let's start by laying some foundational truths about God.

1. God loves us and wants us to be like Him.

And we, who with unveiled faces all reflect the Lord's glory, are being transformed into his likeness with ever-increasing glory, which comes from the Lord, who is the Spirit. (2 Cor. 3:18)

As Christians, we should reflect God's glory because we love Him. Our love for Him should cause a desire within us to know Him better—for it is only through knowing Him that we can begin to love Him. The evidence of our love is our desire to become like Him and be further transformed daily—this is truly proof of our love.

I realize that not everyone had an earthly father who was a good example, so it may be difficult for you to see a loving heavenly father. If you are one of those people, then I suggest you think of someone else that you admire.

I was very fortunate to have a good example as a father, although he has told me on a few occasions that he did not think he was a good example in some areas. However, as I grew up, I found myself becoming more like him. I catch myself all the time imitating him in mannerisms, like in the way I laugh or what I laugh about. It is not something I am actually conscious of; it is just a result of loving him and having spent time with him. Being like him is involuntary—it is just who I have become.

In the same manner in which we become like our earthly fathers, we also become more like our heavenly Father. Although it is nice to have reminders like WWJD (What Would Jesus Do), I really think that when we are transformed we do not need the reminders anymore.

I never, in all my years, said to myself, *OK, what would my dad do in this situation?* I didn't need to; I have become so much like him that I do not need to remind myself to be like him; I just am. I think the same thing happens when we love God—we become like Him because we love Him. We cannot be transformed into our heavenly father's likeness without spending a lot of time with Him. Or, as I have often said, you cannot become like Him unless you know what He is like.

I am sure you have also heard the banker's example. I am not sure if this is true anymore, but it used to be said that bankers were taught to recognize a counterfeit bill by being put in a room with tons of non-counterfeit money. The more a new banker handled the real bills, the more he or she knew the true bills. After the trainee handled real bills for a long period of time, a counterfeit would be introduced, without the trainee's knowledge. Immediately he or she would know which one was counterfeit because he or she had spent so much time getting to know the look and feel of the genuine bills. I have always liked this illustration because it seems to correlate to our knowing Christ and His teachings. We can only spot the fake if we have spent enough time with the Truth. The only way to truly know God is to spend time getting to know Him. Imitating someone is the greatest form of love.

So—do you really love Him? If so, then you are probably reading His Word, His love letter to you, and pursuing a deeper knowledge and understanding of who He is.

2. God's purpose for us individually is that we are transformed into His image.

This means to become less and less like ourselves and more and more like Him every day. This requires sacrifice and change that can sometimes be uncomfortable. But God is glorified by our transformation.

I'll bet you can just guess what is next; it seems so simple. If God instituted marriage and His purpose for us is that we become like Him, then...

3. The purpose of marriage is to change us or transform us into God's likeness.

Some of you are thinking, *But what about companionship, romance and many other reasons for getting married?* Sure there are other reasons, but the other reasons are not the ones people usually forget, which is the reason I am writing this book. During pre-married counseling, I usually make a point of sharing with couples that I think they should write their own vows. Then I go on to suggest they include something like this:

I _____ take you _____ to be my husband/wife. I will accept all conflict between us as God's way of stretching me, molding me, and making me into His image. No matter how uncomfortable I may be, no matter how difficult it becomes, I will choose to open my heart and mind to change and learn from God through every experience. I will not blame you for everything that goes wrong, but instead I will acknowledge God's perfect plan and His desire to use you to make me a godly man/woman. I will try each day to follow God's example in His sacrifice for us on the cross and put aside my desires for your benefit and consider your needs above my own. This is my vow, and with all that I am in Christ and all that He has given me, I will honor you all the days of my life.

4. God wants to use our spouses as tools to make us into the men or women He wants us to be.

Remembering this daily has stopped lots of arguments in my home. I've found that most of the time the battle is not so much against my wife as it is about wanting my way.

After I taught a pre-married counseling program, one man wrote:

James,

I have something that I didn't really get answered that sometimes scares me into thinking, *What if?* But I always wonder, if God made a man and a woman to be together, why is it so difficult? Why do we have to go through pre-marital counseling? Shouldn't it just work? And every time I hear an older couple or anyone say they went through a rocky time in their marriage, I get scared because I don't want that to happen to me. All these things make me wonder if single people have these problems? I dunno...

We miss you guys too and will be keeping in touch more regularly and look forward to our meetup! Can't wait for all this wedding stuff to be over so we can all meet more frequently. Talk to you soon. —E.

E, you ask an excellent question—it is the reason that I am writing a book on marriage.

God's purpose for marriage is to change us to be more like Him. His desire is that during our difficulty we will turn to Him. The pain and difficulty come from our differences. But let me be clear: we do not have to suffer the pain; it does not have to be difficult. It is our choice and stubbornness that cause the difficulty and pain. If we would go quietly and not struggle against the change, then we would be better off. It is our resistance to change that causes difficulty. Many years ago, I read a book called *The Calvary Road* by Roy Hession.* In that book

---

* Hession, *The Calvary Road*. Available at http://www.christianissues.biz/pdf-bin/sanctification/thecalvaryroad.pdf.

there is one part that I can almost recite by memory, but I will quote the book in honor of the author.

People imagine that dying to self makes one miserable. But it is just the opposite. It is the refusal to die to self that makes one miserable.

Dying to self is how we give God permission to change us. It is only then that He can fill us with His character. In the same way, we each must accept our spouse as God's provision and allow Him to use that spouse to transform us.

People get married for so many reasons; the most common reason is they are in love. It is true that two people should not get married if they are not in love. So, love is a valid reason, but what exactly is love? And if love is the reason to get married, then what happens when you don't feel it anymore? There has to be something else. Or maybe our definition of love is the culprit. If love is a feeling, then obviously it's not enough to keep a couple together.

Another one of my favorite books on the topic of love is *Love is a Decision* by Gary Smalley and John Trent.* Even the title is the answer. Some days you may feel love toward your spouse and other days you may not, but if it is a decision, then it doesn't matter how you feel; it's a choice. But wait; if it is just a choice, then you can easily make another choice to not love him or her. So let's use the word *commitment* or, even better, a word that reminds me of another great book, *Covenant Marriage* by Gary Chapman.** A covenant does not have an ending date or terms like a contract. In Bible times, a covenant was often sealed with

---

* Smalley and Trent, *Love is a Decision.*
** Chapman, *Covenant Marriage.*

blood, a symbol of life and death. Often couples headed towards divorce can cite what they would consider the terms of marriage; i.e., "I'm not happy," "I'm not in love anymore," "My needs are not being met," "We are too different," etc. If these were the terms, then we would even have a problem with the definition of the words *happiness* and *love*. We'd have to define a *need* as opposed to a *want*. We'd have to ask, "Are differences bad?" and "How different is 'too different'?"

As you can see, the differences are part of God's plan to transform us into His image. When we experience the differences, we can either fight or let God speak to us. The choice is ours.

I love it when people ask such great questions. Jesus said, "You do not have because you do not ask" (James 4:2 NKJV). This verse is sometimes quoted regarding money or material things, but I believe it is also about our faith and understanding of God. We really should ask more questions and look to find the answers in the scriptures as well as seek out counsel from godly men and women. We usually talk too much and do not listen very well. I catch myself regularly and hear a gentle but firm "Be quiet; be still, I'll take it from here" from the One who has all the answers.

Almost every time I sit together with couples struggling in their marriages, I hear accusations and finger-pointing comments which tell all of us that both individuals are focused on how the other is not meeting their needs. Very rarely do I hear confessions, apologies, and commitment-filled comments. By nature we seem to want to change everyone around us to be like us or see things the way we do. It is natural to think you are right. But if God wants us to be transformed into His image, then we are obviously flawed and are not as "right" as we think we are.

Another thought is that if we are so right, then why do we tend to pick spouses that are so unlike us? I think it is in our makeup. We are imperfect, and true fulfillment will come only when we experience the differences and find we are lacking.

Obviously, we are not fulfilled; we are not complete. I'm sure you have heard the very well-intended comment "You complete me." Well, the truth is that no person can complete us. This is a job exclusively held by your loving heavenly Father. Now, before you get upset with me, I do believe that God can use our spouses to meet our needs, but that is the point: we should never forget the Source. God made him or her for you; therefore, He is the one meeting your needs. I hope you believe this, because if you do, then you will know Whom to turn to next time you feel your needs are not being met. If we could remember this concept and commit it to memory, then there would be a lot less finger-pointing in our marriages. Instead, we will focus our attention on God and ask Him to meet our needs. God's desire is that we seek Him, so we will be accomplishing two things by using this approach. We will have less blaming and arguments with our spouses, and we will draw closer to God by seeking Him. Simply put, we need to do a lot less horizontal pointing and engage in a lot more vertical pointing. We need to point to our Creator and acknowledge first that His will for us is perfect. He knows your spouse and His grace is enough to get you through any disagreement or difference.

Some may say, "This sounds good, but I did not have a good relationship with God when I met my spouse; therefore, this does not apply to me. I just made a bad choice and God would not want this for anyone."

OK, if this is you, I would ask you:

- Do you believe that God is all-powerful?
- Is He still in control?
- Was He surprised by your choice?
- Could He have stopped it, even though you were not listening to Him at the time?

These are just a few questions to make you think.

Please forgive me if you are in a physically harmful marriage. I would encourage you to protect yourself by removing yourself from harm's way and getting help immediately.

Most marriages (even the ones with physical abuse) begin to follow a negative direction with the little things. When the little things are not dealt with, they grow, and the longer it takes for a couple to get help and deal with issues, the worse it gets. I am not sure why many couples keep stuffing everything under the rug. Avoiding the issues does not make them go away, and the assumption that some make is that the other one is the only one avoiding issues. Others won't stuff the issues but will only try to deal with their spouse's issues and not their own issues.

So how does this happen? Let's just take the perfect marriage for example. OK, so that doesn't exist, I agree. But let's just say for this example that there is a couple that is very close to perfect and doing everything right. They both love God very much, they are respected by everyone, and everyone considers them the perfect example. They pray together every day. Daily they are learning things about themselves and changing to be more like Christ. They are so in love in every way, yet very realistic. They never argue... Anyhow, you get the picture. Now, if there is such a couple, how is it possible for them to ever get to the point of divorce? No matter where you are on the perfectometer scale, the answer is the same. It is the little things. No couple ever goes to bed one night with a good, God-centered marriage and then wakes up the next day and says, "I want a divorce." It's a progression of sin so slight that some have compared it with the frog in a pot of water on the stove under low heat. He never even knows what is happening until it is too late. Now, I have not tried this, but this is what I am told and it makes sense.

I know how this feels, as I am sure you do also. I am sure you can remember times when you thought everything was going well, and all of a sudden—bam!—it hits you. Your spouse says something, and you react; he or she reacts in return, and before you know it, you are in a flat out brawl saying things you don't even mean. If your connection to the Author of Marriage is just weak and not completely lost, which requires a complete spiritual reboot, then you might catch yourself and say, "What are we even arguing about?" I can't tell you how many times this has happened to me. Every time I am embarrassed and think, *How did I let that happen?* I love God and I truly want to be used by Him to make my wife feel loved. The spirit is willing, but the flesh is weak. But what an amazing gift we have; unlike the frog, we have been given an awareness to know what is going on. The awareness is the Spirit of God, and the connection we have to our spirit is through faith in His Son Jesus and all that He did on the cross for us. We only have to stay connected to Him through prayer and confession to retain the power and strength to resist the need to protect ourselves and abandon our spouses. So, if it is truly the little things that start this progression towards divorce, how do we protect our family unit from these lies?

The only answer is to consciously start every day by spiritually putting on the full armor of God. Pray individually and pray together. My wife and I find it easier to pray in the evening. As I write this, I am struck with the reality that this is my preference, not hers. As hard as it may be for me, I will try to make a point of getting up with her in the morning and praying together at least part of the time.

Maybe every morning?

OK, I hear You, Lord, but I will need Your help. Do You know how difficult mornings are for me?

Yes, I hear you; that is a true example of sacrifice.

And that is what I am writing about, after all.

Now, if I can only make it seem pleasant, then God will get the glory.

Truly, God, You are going to have to help me here. It is not in me at all.

Wow, this is great! Even if no one ever buys this book or reads these pages, God has already done what He wants to do in me!

Even though I am having a struggle with the timing of our prayers, my wife and I have been pretty consistent in our prayer life. Even with the armor of prayer, we have had challenges. I don't want to imagine how much more challenging they would have been without it.

Seeking God through prayer together every day is the best advice anyone can give you. As we pray together, we are agreeing with God that He is first and that our relationship with Him is a priority and that it is the foundation of our relationship with each other. We also agree together that we will rely on Him to meet our needs and not blame each other when our needs are not met.

I encourage you to begin praying together every day. If you miss a day, don't beat yourself up; just keep pressing on toward the mark as Paul says:

> I press toward the mark for the prize of the high calling of God in Christ Jesus. (Phil. 3:14)

Praying together about your needs will prove to be very helpful. It will be even more effective if you can acknowledge before God and your spouse your failures.

I would like to present this challenge to you. Begin each day on your knees asking God to forgive you for your sins, and then turn to your spouse and ask them to forgive you. Tell them you know you have failed them and that you will try even harder to love them as God loves them. Try it. You will be amazed at what God will do.

PRAYING WITH EYES WIDE OPEN

During a recent family vacation, God gave me some much needed inspiration about prayer that I believe might be helpful as you pursue developing your prayer life together. Let's take a peek into what I journaled to you, my reader, during our vacation experience!

Just moments ago, I was sitting outside on a wooden bench made of split logs that match the cabin I am sitting in now as I write this. I did not sit alone on that bench; I sat there with my lovely wife, Cindy, whom I have grown to love so much more this year. I would like for you to experience what I have experienced here in the Rocky Mountains sitting on that bench. Now I realize it would not have been so special and intimate if you all would have been here with me, but I hope that you can enjoy this even if just through my words! I feel that God wants to use my story to tug at your heart strings as He has mine.

We were sitting on this bench, exhausted from several trips down the hill in front of us on a sled. It took a few moments to catch our breath, something that is quite difficult at this altitude. After several moments of silence—except for the wind and our progressively slower breathing—my wife said, "Let's pray."

I, of course, love to pray, as I have become very fond of my Savior, and, in fact, I had just been thinking how beautiful His creation was, but for some reason it came as a surprise this time. Then as I began to prepare as usual, I started to close my eyes, and it was as if God reached down from the heavens and grabbed my heart and said, "No need to close your eyes this time, my son. You are already focused on me." So, as my wife began to thank our Creator, I continued to gaze at His breathtaking creation. The troubles of the year that she spoke of seemed so far away, and as she asked God to help us through them in the coming year, I felt the peace of God surround me. The wind swirled and I saw wisps of snow dancing like ghosts over the surface of the snow drifts with nowhere to go, and then—just as suddenly—they were gone. I felt God answering her prayers immediately, and He was giving me an answer. He was saying, "You see the wisps of dancing snow? You see how quickly they just fly away? They are here for just a moment. The cold will always come and go, but as that cabin behind you with its warmth waits for you if you find you were not prepared for the amount of cold that comes your way, so I am always here for you with my arms open wide, and, when you are ready, we can sit by the fire and talk for a while..."

Somehow, even with my eyes open, I did not miss a single word of my wife's prayer, and I also received a loving hug from my heavenly Father.

I have always believed in closing my eyes during prayer so as not to be distracted, but there was nothing to distract me there. If not for a distant airplane in the bright blue sky etching its trail to who-knows-where, I could have forgotten about the rest of the world. To me it is clear that sometimes it is best to close our eyes when we pray, but I think we should also look for times when we are not distracted to open our eyes while we pray.

If you are just too easily distracted, I would suggest that at least you can open your eyes metaphorically. Open your eyes so you can see what God is doing, so you can see His plan—His way, not yours. Open your eyes and look, expecting Him to answer your prayers. Remember the scripture that talks about our faith, if we would only have faith as small as a mustard seed then we could move mountains? Really? Did God mean that we could actually move one of the mountains I was looking at in the Rockies? I think what He is trying to impress on us is that He is not limiting us; we limit ourselves. Oh, how little faith we have and what an amazing and gracious Father.

The fading line of the overhead plane was a reminder to me

that the time we would have there to recuperate was only for a little while. In a few days, after we had completely felt God's love and peace, we would return to our home life where there are others who need to feel God's love and acceptance, others who are not as fortunate to experience retreat. That is why we are here; that is why God put us here on earth to share the love of Christ. I know you know that, but if you are like I am, it doesn't take long to be distracted by our own problems; I guess that is why it is an expression of love, because it requires sacrifice. If you need some help with this concept, then I suggest you do a study of what Jesus went through when He made a choice to sacrifice His life for us. After all, He is our strength and our example.

The fading evidence that a plane had passed overhead also reminded me that God does not care as much about where we have been except for us to learn from it (no condemnation). He cares much more about where we are headed. If we could only forgive ourselves and others and forget the past as our heavenly Father forgives and forgets, then we could face the future with more confidence. We can let the failures of the past cripple us—a fear based on the past can destroy our future.

I want you to pause for a moment, take your time, and think about what holds you back. Now let it fade away just as the trail of an airplane fades to leave only blue sky. The clear blue sky is what your Father wants you to see—limitless possibilities. He wants your dreams to come true!

When you fail, He will forgive you again, and just like a giant Etch-a-Sketch, He will give you the clear blue sky. Why do we have such a hard time believing that? I'll let you think about your view of your Creator; you will have to answer Him. Why don't you believe that He loves you and that His love is not full of all the things He doesn't want you to do, but instead all the things He wants for you? He does not want you to settle, He wants you to go for the mountain—and not just any mountain, He wants you to climb the mountain of faith. But before we can climb the mountain of faith, we need to ask Him to remove the obstacles. The most common obstacles to climbing the mountain of faith are related to the wounds we have received. Climbing the mountain, fighting the fight, pressing on toward the mark, and running the race as if to win are all ways of saying we need to believe in ourselves and what God has given us. We need to keep pushing ourselves to greatness. The greatness is God's will for us. He wants us to run the race even though it has already been won. He wants us to press on even though He is already celebrating our arrival.

But I am getting ahead of myself now because, in reality, the obstacles cannot be ignored. We are wounded. We do not believe this stuff. There are many reasons we don't, but one is the lack of forgiveness or, better worded, our lack of understanding of forgiveness. Forgiveness is the foundation of the climb. We cannot be sure of solid footing if we have not dealt with forgiving ourselves or others.

Chapter 3

FOUNDATION OF FORGIVENESS

I F THE PURPOSE of marriage is to further God's transforming work in us, then let's explore the qualities of God and evaluate how well we are doing in our efforts to be more like Him.

One of the most awesome foundational truths about God is His unconditional and complete forgiveness of our sins.

Before I get started on the topic of forgiveness, let me make it clear that our goal is to pursue Christlikeness. But no matter how hard we try, there are some things about Him that we will never be able to understand or imitate. However, He still calls us to pursue understanding and transformation. One example is His ability to forget our past sins. It usually takes much prayer for us to not use past sins against others as ammunition, manipulation, or leverage to get something we want. I will include a real life example here, not about one of the couples I counsel, but about myself. I want you to know that even though I am writing about the way it should be, I struggle just as much or more than you do. But I will not give up! And I do not want you to give up either—which is the reason I share the following with you.

BUT YOU'RE WRONG!

OK, so I don't always do as I say. I am sure anyone who knows me is really shocked. Ha. The truth is I really do believe this stuff, but in the words of Paul, "The spirit is willing and the flesh is weak."

So now to bare my soul and admit my failures to all of you on paper, forever as a record of what happens when we don't keep our eyes on Jesus.

My wife and I had an interesting evening. We had just met with one of our pre-married couples and discussed many of the things that I should have practiced later that evening. On our way home, I reminded her that we still had plans for the evening.

I want even now to identify where she was wrong in her response. I still have a full arsenal and want so bad to blast her even as I write this. So as my struggle begins it is similar to Paul's struggle with sin; I think I have to go through it anyway.

> I do not understand what I do. For what I want to do I do not do, but what I hate I do. And if I do what I do not want to do, I agree that the law is good. As it is, it is no longer I myself who do it, but it is sin living in me. (Rom. 7:15-17)

As I take my first intelligent look back, I am thinking I didn't do anything wrong. We had just finished spending a great evening with encouraging words and uplifting comments. We were driving home and I mentioned that I was looking forward to spending some intimate time with her. Whatever it was she said, I felt rejection. What a horrible feeling—although I remember brushing it off. So far, I was responding the way I teach others to. Then we got home and I jumped into the shower and I started talking to her about some of my financial goals, including reduction of debt. Still my heart was OK. I truly was having this conversation as an assurance that we would climb back quickly from the damage of the previous year. Somehow, she did not hear that. She started pointing horizontally. Once again I was rejected. I know clearly that I have made some mistakes that have led to loss of money in our family bank account. It already bothers me that I have failed her. For her to bring up my mistakes was just wrong. But it's not my job to point back. Nevertheless, I did. The flesh is weak and wounded; I reacted to the pain. I retaliated by instinct, like an animal that has been injured bites back even if you are trying to help it. Either because of growth or decline, I am not sure which, I left the room. I used to insist that she talk about it right there before going to sleep, in spite of the fact that she is not a night person.

I retreated to my hammock outside, expecting any minute for her to emerge and apologize. Why shouldn't she? She was clearly wrong. She had rejected me, humiliated me, and blamed me for years of mistakes. Were they even mistakes? More like investments that were not profitable. I felt myself preparing for a battle that I knew I would win. I started searching through the cabinets of my mind for ammunition. I found some and remembered where I put a whole box of ammo. I started towards that door and then the pain of my wounds distracted me and the truth about myself cut me again as if the blade was still stuck in my back. It was my fault; the things she said were true. But wait a minute; I did not do anything to intentionally hurt us. God could have stepped in at any time. He had allowed this. If He allowed it, then there is something He wants her to learn. (Smile.) After all, I sought God daily on the decisions I made. If He allowed these things to happen to our economy and personally to our financial status, then there was something more important than the money. Remembering the financial classes at church, I acknowledged that it all belongs to God, and if He wants to take some away, then who are we to complain? I waited. She never came outside.

Now I was really mad. I surprised myself—I have never been an angry person. But I mentally started moving towards the ammo cabinet.

How could she sleep? How insensitive! Didn't she know the damage she had caused? That is just wrong! To deliver wounds like that and then peacefully go to dreamland as if nothing had happened at all? She must not have a heart. How else would you explain this? She can't be sleeping well. I am sure God will give her nightmares to help her realize how wrong she is.

Still nothing. It was quiet, about midnight now. As I continued the battle in my mind, I gathered ammunition; I looked for just the right thing to say, maybe the hollow point bullet, which, when it hits, separates and has incredible knockdown power. *That's what I need, and I know right where they are.* As I mentally started towards that cabinet, I thought, *Interesting that they call it a hollow point. It does a lot of damage, but there really is nothing to it.*

I know: I'll send her some witty texts on her phone. She will wake up and realize she should come apologize.

Still nothing.

She either saw them and is being completely selfish by ignoring them, or she is sleeping so peacefully because she has no conscience at all. Why does she want to always have someone to blame? Why does it always seem to be me? After all, life is not perfect. We won't know perfect until we see Jesus again. She is definitely barking up the wrong tree with me. I know I am not perfect. I mean, none of us are, right?

Oh yeah, I've just found a real powerful round. Remember the verse that talks about taking the beam out of your eye so you can see clearly to take the speck out of your brother's eye? I'll text something like that to her. If she is awake, she will surely realize she has a beam in her eye and come to me.

I waited, getting a little tired, but still too worked up to sleep, still feeling pain from my wounds like I had been shot with rock salt. It stung. For a fleeting moment, I thought it would have been better to receive a final blow instead of these flesh wounds that hurt so much.

Wounds to my flesh? Hmmm, sounds like something from the Bible. Something about the flesh dying...

I was still too hurt to know where that was coming from.

That's it. I don't need to blow her away with my words; I just need to cause her pain like she did to me.

Something about not retaliating flashed through my mind, but I dismissed its annoying tug, still not sure what that was about.

OK, I am exhausted. I guess she is not coming. I will let her know that I will be unavailable tomorrow to help her with anything. Maybe that will sting a little. I'm sure I will think of something more in the morning.

Embarrassed for a second by my thoughts, I had a new, somewhat convicting thought: *That does not sound like me, or does it? Maybe the old me. Who can tell the difference when you are wounded and tired? I'll keep preparing for the battle in the morning. I hope I don't forget where I put all my ammunition, but I am sure I will find more in the morning.*

I lay down in the bed next to my wife, not trying to be quiet as I usually am.

Maybe she'll waken and I can lie, saying, "Sorry for waking you."

I lay there rigid in my place, determined not to lose the ammo I had found. As I faded, I felt my grasp loosen, and I finally felt my mind release my weapons.

I awoke with a jolt! I listened. Unusually awake, I thought of preparing for the battle.

How could I have let myself sleep? Oh yeah, that was going to be my first blow. She's walking by now. If she knows I am awake, then she will ask if I will still help her this morning. No, she needs to know she cannot treat me that way and then get a good night of sleep and expect everything to be OK in the morning. Why does that stuff not bother her? She must not care about me at all. She definitely cares more about sleep than she does about me.

As I found the ammo cabinet in my mind again, I added to that and said to myself, *She obviously cares more about money and our financial future than she does about our relationship.* This was very evident to me based on the pain I felt from the wounds I received the night before.

I think I wounded her by not waking up or appearing like I wasn't awake. If she doesn't notice all that I do, I will just stop doing that stuff. I'll start by not making the bed. That probably won't work. She won't notice since I have not been very good at this lately.

For a second I thought, *Maybe I have not been doing a good job at showing her I love her. . .*

None of that matters right now. I just need to find my ammunition. I just can't seem to remember anything. Mornings are not very good for me. I am having trouble remembering why I am angry. I know she did something. I still feel the pain; I'm just not sure how it happened, like a bruise you get and not sure where it came from.

Whew! Finally, she is gone.

I got up and noticed I had lost even more weight. I had been trying to lose, having said to others that my wife deserves less of me, physically and spiritually. I was really starting to wake up.

I have my men's business lunch group today; I am not sure what I will talk about.

Driving around doing errands and thinking I needed to work, I was just not in the mood. I told myself it was all her fault anyway, so I had her to blame for having a non-productive day.

Oh, no, I completely missed a morning appointment!

I arrived early at lunch and thought I would work a little on my book, but that was not the result.

After sharing with the guys some of what I had experienced, I realized after about thirty minutes or so that I could have stopped the whole disagreement by not being so selfish. If I had only stopped to think about what I know about my lovely wife, I would have known that she likes her beauty sleep. (I have carefully chosen to use the word *likes* instead of needs beauty sleep because she truly is a beautiful woman inside and out.) I should have known that we went a little late in our meeting. I should have known that after 11 PM she is not interested in having a long conversation. I should have known after fifteen years that when she gets tired, she says things she does not mean. I should have known her better. This is my sin. The sin that started it all.

I could then think of lots of verses that should have come to me the night before, like these:

> Do nothing out of selfish ambition or vain conceit, but in humility consider others better than yourselves. (Phil. 2:3)

> Likewise, ye husbands, dwell with them according to knowledge, giving honour unto the wife, as unto the weaker vessel, and as being heirs together of the grace of life; that your prayers be not hindered. (1 Pet. 3:7 KJV)

I should have known. Nothing else matters. It does not matter what she did—that is between her and God. God wants to change me. And today I think He did. I will remember. I will commit to memory which cabinet holds the flower vase instead of the ammunition.

I wanted to share this with you as an example of how things can get if we do not seek God first each and every day. Sometimes it only takes a moment for us to lose focus. We must stay connected to the vine: "I am the vine; you are the branches. If a man remains in me and I in him, he will bear much fruit; apart from me you can do nothing" (John 15:5).

If I could only forgive as He does. He forgives us immediately upon the thought of confession as seen in 1 John 1:9. Also, in true character, He chooses to forget as seen in this psalm: "As far as the east is from the west, so far has he removed our transgressions from us" (Ps. 103:12).

When I was about seventeen years old, this verse took on new meaning for me and I learned not to take the Word of God for granted. I was living in Venezuela with my parents, who were missionaries there to a tribal group called the Panares. I had developed a very strong relationship with one of the boys I grew up with. Tose and I were sitting one day at his house in hammocks since there were no chairs and the floor was dirt. We had been talking about some of the struggles he was having, and he mentioned that some of his people were really not living lives that would honor God. I immediately thought of a passage in Timothy where Paul challenged him to not let anyone look down on him because of his youth. Tose did not seem to know what I was talking about, as I mentioned the book of Timothy. He showed me his Bible and, sure enough, the book of Timothy was not in it yet.

At lunchtime, I returned home and asked my mother, who was the primary translator for the Panare Bible, about the passage in Timothy.

"Haven't you translated Timothy yet?" I asked her.

"No," she answered. "It is not completed. In fact, I have been working on that very chapter."

I was so excited! Here I had a chance to show my friend a portion of the Bible for the very first time. My mom printed out a copy of the portion and gave it to me. I went back to my friend's house and excitedly showed him the passage I was referring to.

He, too, was excited and said, "This morning I did not know that. I did not know that part of God's Word. But now I do."

We continued to talk about God's love and forgiveness, and then I quoted Psalm 103:12. He said he did not quite understand it. He had some basic understanding that the world was round and he also understood east and west, but there was something still unclear about it.

So I picked up a nearby rock and said, "Imagine this is the world. If you were to travel north..." I motioned in an upward direction on the rock "...at some point you would reach the top and begin to head south." Then I indicated an orbital direction around the rock saying, "If you were to travel east around the world..." I pointed down the trail behind his house "in *that* direction for many years, one day you would come from the opposite direction as I pointed. Even then, you would pass the point where we sit now and go back down the path behind your house again. You can travel east forever and never make it to west."

He nodded with a smile.

Then I said, "That is how far God removes our sin from us. He chooses to forget."

You see, God does not keep records of wrongs or use our past to make us do as He wishes. And here is another one—would you forgive someone if you knew they would do the same thing again? God forgives you even though He knows the future and knows that you are going to repeat the same behavior.

Some of you have not forgiven yourselves for something, and others have not been able to bring themselves to forgive someone else. I am going to discuss both of these aspects of forgiveness. Obviously Jesus is our perfect example, and we are supposed to learn from how He forgives us. A study of Jesus is always helpful for us to understand Him better.

My wife is sitting in a chair right now, just a few feet away, reading an excellent book by Charles Swindoll that profiles Jesus. Jesus—if we could only be like Him, then we would not have any trouble forgiving ourselves or others.

Before I write a few of my own thoughts about forgiving as Christ forgives us, I want to discuss the practical aspects of forgiveness.

First, let me say that if you are the one who has not forgiven yourself for something, then I would like to challenge you to think about the sacrifice Jesus made for you on the cross so that you could be forgiven. Was it enough? Do you believe He has forgiven you? If He has forgiven you, as I know He has, then by not forgiving yourself you are not accepting His sacrifice as enough. I understand that the circumstances or consequences of your behavior may sometimes make it hard to forget or forgive. But God is God, and you are not. If He has forgiven you, then you will need to accept.

As the title of this chapter indicates, forgiveness is a foundational necessity to have a healthy marriage. You can not build a marriage without it. There are various reasons why we are not as forgiving of our spouses as we should be.

One reason we do not forgive is because we are at times a little self righteous and in our hearts we have judged the behavior of our spouse based on the thought that we are better than they are in that area. In fact this is the reason and foundation for our judging and unforgiving heart.

First let me say that, even though our reason for judging them and not forgiving them is that we are stronger in that area, does not make us perfect or beyond being tempted.

> No temptation has seized you except what is common to man. And God is faithful; he will not let you be tempted beyond what you can bear. But when you are tempted, he will also provide a way out so that you can stand up under it. (1 Cor. 10:13)

Even if there is one area where you are stronger, it is a fact that there are areas that you are weak in and need to be forgiven. Not recognizing your own weaknesses will by nature make you a more judging and less forgiving person. God wants you both at the same place, He wants you both to acknowledge your sin and weaknesses and seek forgiveness from Him. He is the only true judge. He is the only one who has a right to judge us. When you both agree before God where you fall short, then He can use you in mighty ways in your spouse's life.

Not being forgiving or gracious of others is an abuse or misunderstanding of God's grace and forgiveness of us.

Some personalities will have more difficulty forgiving. For example, someone who has the personality traits of a prophet type will have very strong opinions of right and wrong as well has how things should be done. The downside is that, when people do not do things as they would do them, they may have trouble being gracious and forgiving. The upside is that these people will have great impact on others for good and will challenge others to walk closer to God and do what is right.

Another reason we have trouble forgiving is that we feel that if we don't make them pay they will just repeat the behavior. And we unintentionally take on God's role as judge as I illustrated in my previous story.

Although there are probably many other reasons to not forgive, the final one I want to share is that at times we justify not forgiving because our offender did not ask for forgiveness or acknowledge their offense. This is illustrated in the following story.

If you are having trouble forgiving someone else because they never ask, then I think my struggles this past year may be helpful for you. You see, I have always been a forgiving person. I suppose it is because I know how much forgiveness I need, and therefore, when someone needs to feel Christ's forgiveness from someone here on earth, I am happy to share with them the wonders of how our Savior forgives.

But here is where the problem began for me. I had a year where my trust in someone (not my wife) was abused. This person caused much difficulty in my life. I will not go into great detail, as I do not think it is relevant, but I have to admit I struggled with being able to forgive that person. I have always thought that if anyone were to ask for my forgiveness I would offer it freely, but I have always made this conditional on one word: *ask*. If they ask, I will forgive them. But the time went by, and that person didn't ask me to forgive him. There was no asking, and I stood strong on the verse: "If we confess our sins, He is faithful and just and will forgive our sins and purify us from all unrighteousness" (1 John 1:9).

I was trying to model what God does, or so I thought. One day as I was struggling with this, I realized that it was really damaging me. I was no longer writing, I was not doing some of the ministry things I so much enjoyed, and I was just waiting for the person to ask for forgiveness. And then it hit me. This person may never ask, and it did not seem to bother them at all. I was the only one who was hurt. The thought came to me with a resounding "DUH!" I should have known this.

The verse that I loved still bothered me, and then I realized that God's forgiveness is always available. It is not conditional, based on whether or not we ask, but the confession is for us— it is sort of an acceptance of what He has already done. I also thought of a passage when Jesus was dying on the cross. He said, "Father, forgive them; for they know not what they do" (Luke 23:34). So He does forgive, even if we are not aware of our sin. It is only when we confess, agree with Him, and acknowledge our sin that we can enjoy the beauty of forgiveness.

So don't hold back your forgiveness toward others, even if you think they are not worthy of your forgiveness. Holding on to a grudge will only hurt you. If you hold back forgiveness for others or for yourself, you will be held back from pursuing all that God has for you.

And finally some really good reasons to forgive. Forgiveness is healing, When we forgive our spouses we are allowing God's healing work in them and in ourselves. Forgiveness also promotes forgiveness, When we forgive them they are likely to find it easier to forgive us. Forgiveness promotes change. When we forgive each other it allows the focus to change to rebuilding. I am reminded of an experience I had on a recent trip to Haiti after the earthquakes. We were there with a group of doctors and nurses. We were working in a hospital that had survived the quakes. Our mission was to save lives. But if we had noticed significant cracks in the foundation of the building we would not have been able to focus on saving lives. In fact there was a time where we heard predictions of more quakes. The idea that there could be cracks in the foundation that we could not see caused many of us to shift focus to ourselves, and with good reason. If we ignored the underlying possibility, it was possible that our work of saving lives would have ceased.

So please, do not ignore the cracks in the foundation of your marriage. Forgive each other and ask for forgiveness, so you can go on saving the lives of your children or others around you who are watching.

Chapter 4

MOUNTAIN OF FAITH

I AM SURE THAT if I asked you to choose fear or faith, you would not have much trouble deciding. Most of us would not think twice if given this simple choice. So why does it seem to be so hard?

Fear keeps us from pursuing our dreams. The fear of failure keeps us from trying new things; the fear of disappointing others can be very discouraging and can cause us to want to give up. Fear can simply destroy us.

> For God hath not given us the spirit of fear; but of power, and of love, and of a sound mind. (2 Tim. 1:7 KJV)

So why does fear have such a strong grip on us?

The simple answer is that our faith is not strong enough. We believe the lies. We choose fear over faith.

How do we strengthen our faith? We must follow the road of faith: to know, to believe, and to act on our faith.

TO KNOW

First we must KNOW the source of our faith. Our faith needs to be based on who God is and what He says about Himself in His Word. We must have faith in the facts. The strengthening of our faith comes from remembering what God has already done. I suggest keeping a journal as you read through the scriptures and as you see God work in your life.

TO BELIEVE

Secondly, we must BELIEVE what God says!

While I was growing up in Venezuela, South America, I had the amazing privilege of watching and listening as my mother worked at translating the Bible into a tribal language. She would often experience some difficulty because of missing words in the tribal language. The word *believe* was one of the words that did not exist in the native language. After some time working with the people to try to find an alternate way of translating this very important concept, they came up with this definition: "to say in your heart, 'It is true!'" I love that! It is not enough just to say it in your head, but to say it with your heart is to believe.

TO ACT

God has given us all we need, so now we must act without fear and respond to what He has shown us. Don't let fear keep you from pursuing God's plan for you.

We are blessed today in the United States to hear so many

good teachings which were written first in the Bible and then preached to us. We read about how God wants us to act in so many good books. It is not difficult to get the message, but when it comes to putting these things into practice in our lives, it seems that everything we have read and heard is gone. It is because we have not connected with the Author. The Author of Life, the Author of Marriage is Jesus. It is only through the relationship with the Author that the facts become part of us. It is only when we say in our hearts that it is true, that we begin to ACT as though we believe it.

Decide today to choose FAITH, to KNOW Him better, to BELIEVE what He says, and to ACT on your faith. Since we're talking about acting, I want to invite you to take the time to act upon an invitation to email me at james@theauthorofmarriage.com with your questions about marriage, or just to let me know what God is saying to you on the subject of marriage. You can also join my interactive blog at www.TheAuthorofMarriage.com.

Having faith in who God has made you and choosing faith when it comes to pursuing something that He has placed before you is foundational. When I was single and did not have a family, having faith was different. My faith was built on the steps that I had taken, and every time God came through for me, my faith was strengthened. For example, I know that God provides financially for us not only because He says so in His Word but also because I have seen Him provide for my family on the mission field as a child. I also have seen Him provide in miraculous ways for me when I was in Bible college, through gifts from others, some of whom I had never met. The timing of these events and the exact amounts needed were, for me, profound provisions from God.

When I got married, I quickly realized that my faith was not her faith. She did not have the same experiences that I did, and she did not see how God provided for me so many times. I saw my faith take on a whole new life. I now had to have faith in God that He would bring her along in His time. I had to have faith that He would comfort her when I could not. And most profoundly, I realized that I needed to have faith in God's timing. I struggled with the fact that God had given her a free will and that the time it would take for her to learn what I had would make for some very difficult trials while I waited. At some point, I realized that if I was focusing on what God wanted to do in me, then I wouldn't have time to think or worry about how long it would take her. As I think about this now, I realize that God used the time I was waiting to teach me patience. It is also very obvious that He taught me many things by using the differences between Cindy and me. Looking back, it is evident that God had taught her things that I needed to learn from her. Some of those things I have learned from her have been crucial to the person God's made me to be. I know today that I would not have had so many opportunities to minister to others if not for her outgoing and accepting nature. I have watched her, and I have learned what God wanted me to learn. I will continue to watch for years to come because she is quite fascinating, mysterious, and worth pursuing!

One of the reasons we so often choose fear instead of faith is that our faith is wrongly placed in the past and in people. How others have treated us in the past greatly affects our faith. But if this is true, then our faith is not in God.

We cannot do anything to change the past. As discussed earlier, we will need to forgive people from our past who have made it difficult for us to have faith in God. However, we can affect the future of those around us by developing a good balance of confidence and humility.

Have you noticed that when people around us come across as confident, we have a tendency to want to remind them of humility? Our motives may be pure, our intention could be to make sure they understand that the source of our confidence should always be God, but in the process, we are really beating them down. We must be careful to not always identify confidence in others as being self-sufficient or prideful. We have so often heard that pride is wrong and sinful—and rightfully so. I agree that if our source is not Jesus, then it is sinful, and I understand that it is a daily struggle for many of us to give credit to God. But it is also easy to get stuck here in the condemnation: "Therefore, there is now no condemnation for those who are in Christ Jesus" (Rom. 8:1).

You see, there is a good pride, the pride one has in all that God has given him. We should have confidence and be proud to be called children of God. Because He is our source, we need to live in confidence—we need to know that we can do great things for Him because He has given us what we need.

> His divine power has given us everything we need for
> life and godliness (2 Pet. 1:3a)

It is not our job to judge if the confidence in others is of God. It is our job to cheer them on. What if that someone around you has been given gifts by God to be a great man or woman—to be a writer, preacher, counselor, or even the president of the United

States? Perhaps all they need are your words of encouragement to give them wings. What will you do?

Are you regularly encouraging your spouse to pursue his or her talents or dreams? Do you know what your spouse's talents and dreams are?

Some might say we should just know what we are good at and we should not be looking for a pat on the back. They would say, "If we need this encouragement, then we must be performing these tasks as unto man and not unto God." They would say, "If God has called you to do something, then why do you keep asking me if you are doing a good job? Don't you know that God is pleased with all you have to offer? Isn't that enough?"

The truth is that half of our population is motivated and encouraged by simply completing the tasks set before them in day-to-day life. They have already received the confirmation and encouragement needed by the simple satisfaction of the accomplishment. The other half desperately needs the encouragement of the body of believers to spur them on to greatness. Does this somehow make their talents less valuable? Is their need for encouragement really wrong or simply a good use of the talents of others in the body of believers?

I will admit that I am one who needs encouragement. I have a great passion to help people, and the reason is truly because I find joy in serving God in this way. I seek God for direction and for just the right words to use when counseling someone. My desire is to be a conduit to carry God's message to the person sitting in front of me and I ask God to help me as I do so. However, encouragement is kind-of like a road map for me in my ministry that keeps me on track. If I say something or do something that is helpful to someone, a sincere thank-you or positive comment helps me to know if I am headed in the right direction. It helps me know that God was working through me to communicate effectively. Encouragement is like a barometer of how well I am listening to God. I believe this is the way He wants us to be. He does not want us to get direction and then run on our own strength the rest of the time. He wants us to keep checking in to see if we are being effective. For me, the easiest way to check in is to see the expression on someone's face when I speak. The greatest form of encouragement for me is when I have shared some advice that I believe is from God, and the person I am sharing with takes my advice and it changes his or her life for good; he or she is closer to God today because of my willingness to be used. There is nothing more satisfying to me.

Chapter 5

PURSUIT OF HAPPINESS

I AM AMAZED AT how many of the married couples I counsel focus their hearts on happiness. I often hear them say, "I'm just not happy." Maybe someone can show me, but I do not remember happiness being a biblical ingredient in marriage.

I guess when I think about happiness, I think of the things that people usually pursue to make themselves happy. I do not need to list them here, as I know you are very aware of them.

I would hope that the things Christians pursue are different from the things pursued by people without faith in Jesus. But I am afraid there is not as much difference as you or I would be comfortable with.

It is almost impossible to define the word *happiness* without using other words that are similar but, in my opinion, not the same. For example, joy is used to define happiness. If you were to look up both words in a Webster dictionary, you would find the definitions to be very similar; however, I think we tend to use them in very different situations and tend to make our own definitions based on our perceived meaning. It may be that my self-created definition of happiness is the problem or possibly a solution.

Joy seems to be more about choice not circumstances, as we see in this passage of scripture: "Consider it pure joy, my brothers, whenever you face trials of many kinds" (James 1:2). Even when things are not going well, we can have joy. This kind of joy comes only from God. It is also the kind of joy that would see conflict with our spouses as a way to know each other better and to learn more about God and His plan for us. This particular scripture speaks of both happiness and joy: "But may the righteous be glad and rejoice before God; may they be happy and joyful" (Ps. 68:3). If the two words mean the same thing, then why did the translators of the NIV interpret God's word by using them both in this verse? The use of the word *happy* here is evidence that happiness is not all bad.

So why do I have a problem with the pursuit of happiness? I think it is because it seems to be more self-focused than joy. Focusing on ourselves and our needs first is a recipe for a failed marriage.

I suppose that if you were to seek God and only God for this happiness, then the pursuit would be good. However, that is not usually what I hear. What I have heard regarding marriage is "I am just not happy anymore. God would want me to be happy, wouldn't He?" So as we see here, the problem with this is the source of the happiness. This person believes that the marriage relationship is supposed to make them happy. Happiness seems circumstantial; if I don't have something, then I am not happy. If I don't feel loved, then I am not happy. There is usually a circumstance that is the cause for happiness, whereas joy is something you can have even when the circumstances are not good. Joy seems to include the concept of contentment. It is a choice, pure and simple. In fact, it is a command! "Keep your lives free from the love of money and *be content with what you have*, because God has said, 'Never will I leave you; never will I forsake you'" (Heb. 13:5).

He did not just say, "Try to be content." It's almost like we are betraying God if we are not content. The reason we should be content is final and absolute—He is in control; He will never leave you or abandon you. He knows what you need, and He is your provider. To not believe this is to not believe in God. After all, one of God's names is Jehovah Jireh, meaning "The Lord will provide." Let's take a look at the story of Abraham and Isaac on the mountain:

> And Abraham called the name of that place *Jehovahjireh*: as it is said to this day, In the mount of the LORD it shall be seen. (Gen. 22:14, KJV, emphasis added)

> So Abraham called that place *The LORD Will Provide*. And to this day it is said, "On the mountain of the LORD it will be provided." (Gen. 22:14, emphasis added)

But let's look a little deeper into this. He does not always provide in advance. If you read the story, before verse fourteen you will see that God stopped Abraham from killing his son just in time. His timing is perfect. He wants to see how we will respond. He is glorified by our choice to climb, even when we are afraid and are not sure what will happen. Abraham knew God would provide and that God was good, but he did not know that God would spare his son's life. He was climbing the mountain of faith.

Have you climbed your mountain today? The mountain of faith can sometimes be a scary place to be. Fear will creep in and question your faith. Will God really provide? You may not know until the last second. He wants to know if you will follow through even if you believe He may take something from you. What if He does not come through for you? What if He allows the suffering? Can you still climb? Is your faith still strong? Or is it based on your understanding? What if God had not stopped Abraham from killing his son? Would that have made Him cease to be God? We do not understand His ways, or we may not understand why He has allowed things to get as bad as they have. But He is still God and He is testing our faith. Will we grow or will we slide backwards down the mountain? Downhill sounds good sometimes—sometimes it is tempting to simply coast—but if we allow ourselves to coast even for a moment, we may miss God's provision. Like Abraham's story, God will provide the ram in the bush according to His perfect timing.

Talking Like a Foolish Woman

Before you get upset with me about the title of this section, I want to explain. It's directly taken from the book of Job: "He replied, *'You are talking like a foolish woman.* Shall we accept good from God, and not trouble?' In all this, Job did not sin in what he said" (Job 2:10, emphasis added).

It just so happens that in this story the woman was the one

who was not trusting God. This does not mean that men don't have this problem as well. The point is that if we take our eyes off Jesus for even a second and doubt His goodness, then we are foolish.

It is foolish to not accept the bad as well as the good in our lives. Even though we don't like to think about the pain of the bad stuff that happens to us, it is usually later that we realize all that God taught us during that time. It is hard to think about the losses and still keep a positive attitude. You see, we think we know what we need. Many of us have merged the lines between need and want. We really do not trust that God will provide. We can do all the right things and still not get what we want. Although I am writing about marriage, I think that sometimes we need to go back to the basics and allow ourselves to be parented again. So, with that in mind, I want to share with you something that we learned while taking parenting classes about fourteen years ago.

We had been married for about a year and had decided that we wanted to be foster parents. We were expecting our first child and taking classes provided by the foster care system.

One of the most valuable lessons we learned in the course was to identify the needs of the child. These needs were described as follows. The child needs, or has a right to, a roof over his or her head, food, basic clothing, privacy, and a place to sleep. Everything else is a privilege and can be taken away at any time.

It is foolish to expect to have all that we want. God knows that obtaining all we want will not satisfy us. True satisfaction comes from investing inwardly. Investing inwardly is being willing to take the time to read and to discuss our hearts with our spouses without any blame. Investing inwardly often requires sacrifice, but the rewards are more precious than silver. The only investment that will always have a good return is the investment in relationships. The most solid of these investments is our relationship with God and the second is our relationship with our spouse.

I really don't like "what ifs," especially when they seem to be focused on the worst possible outcome. I suppose this is a personality trait, but I also believe that we are called to think on "whatever is lovely."

Finally, brothers, whatever is true, whatever is noble, whatever is right, whatever is pure, whatever is lovely, whatever is admirable—if anything is excellent or praiseworthy—think about such things (Phil. 4:8).

However, it is sometimes helpful for the purpose of inward investments—contentment, joy or happiness—to consider the value of life based on a "what if" question.

So, what if you were to wake up tomorrow in a house filling with smoke? The first thing you think about is your family. You rush to get them all out of the house and are relieved that everyone is OK. Your house burns to the ground with your cars in the garage and you later hear that insurance will not cover the loss due to some clause you were unaware of. While sitting at a nearby restaurant with your family, trying to figure out what to do next, you get a phone call from your boss explaining that the economy has taken its toll on his business and he needs to let you go. You start to beg for your job, but you get interrupted by gasps from other customers who are now gathering around a television. The reporter says we have been attacked again in at least ten major cities. The reporter tries to maintain composure but fails as he says, "The stock market is crashing like never before.

It's over folks! Life as we know it is over." What if this were to happen to you? Would your value system change? What would be important to you then? The reason I wanted to take this emotional journey with you is for you to consider how you invest your time. What did you spend your money on last month? Did you spend it on things that can be lost in the fire?

My desire here is to help you to prepare for the bad, be ready to weather the storm, but to focus on the good and all the blessings. As the old song goes, "Count your blessings, name them one by one." Try it. I mean now. Stop reading for a moment and name your blessings out loud...

Do you feel better? If you don't, then I have not done a very good job of helping you to understand what your needs are. Or maybe you should start over and read this again. And take time to look up the verses I have mentioned.

So in conclusion, being happy is a good thing, but it should never be the goal in marriage. Joy, however, can be found if you just look for it. Joy can be found even when you are wrong and your spouse is right. Joy can be found when things are going well and, when life seems to be giving you lemons, joy helps you make lemonade! How sweet it is to know the joy of the Lord!

Chapter 6

PURSUIT OF PERFECTION

ARLY IN OUR marriage, a counselor friend of mine said something to me that made a significant impact on me. I don't remember exactly what he said, but I remember the message God spoke through him. At the time, I sat in his office and shared that I was discouraged because it seemed I could never do enough to please my wife. I felt like I was trying very hard to do what she expected. Sometimes she wouldn't even notice my efforts at all. I felt like giving up. He stopped me and said something like, "Don't let that bother you; she was made to long for perfection. This is good news. It means she is longing for heaven."

Since that day, I have added many things to this message from real life experience. It started with a personal struggle. I thought, *If she is longing for perfection, then I am off the hook because she won't find that in me or any other person on earth.* But just as I felt relief, I realized my responsibility as a husband is to be a godly man who would show the character of Christ. Now the pressure is on again, but wait—that's not something I can do in my power. So the pressure is off again. So all I have to do is yield to Christ in me. Now the battle begins again. because I am not sure I completely trust Him. But—*why not?*

Why don't we trust God completely? The answer is we just don't know Him well enough. Even after all these years, all of the Bible training, and all the amazing things He has done for me, and I still don't completely trust Him? One of the reasons we have difficulty yielding to His will is that we really don't like the idea of giving up our own will. This struggle is the perfecting of our faith. We must choose to trust Him. It will help if we remember all that He has done and that He has never let us down.

I am a little encouraged as I realize that I am in good company. Paul spoke of his struggles to do the right things; even when he genuinely wanted to, he seemed to be unable to. The Israelites did the same. Over and over again God came through in miraculous ways. It didn't take long for them to forget all that He had done for them in the wilderness and begin to complain again. Then God would send a prophet and the people would bow down and praise God. We may think that is absurd, but many of us are guilty of even shorter memories. How many of you had a spiritual revelation last Sunday but today cannot remember exactly what it was that stirred your heart? This is the very reason Jesus said to practice the taking of the elements (communion)—so that we would remember. God knows we have short-term memory problems. He can help us if we ask Him to.

I refuse to forget that God brought my wife and me together

and that He knew what He was doing. She is part of His plan in my life to make me into the man He has called me to be.

Although we should not pursue perfection in others, we are called to pursue the perfecting of ourselves to be more like Jesus. One of the ways this can occur is to agree that God was in control when He allowed you to meet your spouse and that he wants to use the differences to transform you. I have heard many individuals justify their actions because they weren't Christians or were not walking with God when they met their spouses. God being in control is not dependent on whether or not you had a good relationship with Him at the time you met and married your spouse. His plan is perfect! He wants to use every situation to transform you.

DOROTHY AND THE TIN MAN—EMBRACE THE DIFFERENCES

My wife said we were invited to a Halloween party. I have never been a fan of Halloween for lots of reasons, one of which is the fact that I am an introvert. I do not generally like groups, crowds, or parties. Some of you who know me may be a little surprised and say that you do not think I am an introvert. However, I have always defined an introvert as someone who re-energizes by being alone or keeping company with only one or two close friends. Even though I have experienced many changes over the years and have been known to speak in front of large groups, I still look forward to some refreshing time alone before my next group interaction.

God has used my wife over the years to change me in many ways. It is by watching her and by the gentle prodding of the

Holy Spirit that I have become an extrovert by appearance, but I am still an introvert at heart. God impressed on me years ago that my desire to minister to others would not be well served by focusing on just a few people. I was allowing my personal preference to affect how many people I would be able to minister to.

So this year when my wife said we were going to a party with lots of people we didn't know, in an uncharacteristic form I said, "OK!" And I started thinking about how we would dress. After thinking about it for a while, I decided I would be Tin Man and she could be Dorothy. I have always enjoyed finding more ways to use duct tape and so I made my outfit with two rolls of duct tape, attached in overlapping form to a pair of jeans and long sleeve shirt. I then took a funnel and wrapped it in duct tape and did the same for some old shoes. The outfit turned out really great and so did the evening.

We got to spend some time at that party talking with a young couple that had been dating for a while and contemplating marriage. This conversation was God's message to me that all I need to do is show up, and He will provide the ministry opportunities. (By the way, I have found that I can be very energized in a group setting if I get the opportunity to have some meaningful ministry-focused conversation with someone else in the group. In past years, I would have missed out on this type of ministry simply because I call myself an introvert.)

I am pleased to say that Dorothy has given me a new heart! I have become much more like her in the last sixteen years. God sent her to me and it is because of her that others have been helped, encouraged, and ministered to. God knew what I needed when He brought her into my life. I am a much better man and minister than I ever would have been without her.

It is so easy for us to reject the ways of others and to allow our predefined identity to keep us from what God wants. He wants to use us, and there is no room for the excuses of the introvert. It's OK if you are an introvert. This only means that you will always be energized and refreshed by solitude or quality time with a few special people. But it's not OK to use this as a defense against what God has called all of us to do, and that is *to go* into all the world—first to the party in your neighborhood and then to the rest of the world. He wants us to tell everyone we see and meet that He is God and that He loves us and understands us because He is our Creator.

Just in case you extroverts think you're going to get away so easily, let me say that you can sometimes focus a little too much on the number of people you talk to at the party and not enough on the quality of conversation. The job God calls us to everywhere, every day, is to look for opportunities to plant seeds that will grow into a desire to know God better. Every conversation does not need to include a full salvation plan, but there should be seeds planted.

Now, back to the topic of Dorothy and the Tin Man. I am sure I am not alone when I say that it really takes a conscious effort to use the new heart we have been given and to pursue the understanding of our Dorothy. It is natural to want to stay the way we are and to see the differences as negative. We have to really work at seeing the differences as God's design for unity. It seems to often cause the opposite of unity, but that is because we resist the change. We like who we are, and we fight to stay that way.

I used to like going to the same place for vacation, the same restaurant, and I even like to sit in the same place at church.

But God gave me a wife who does not like to go to the same places. We have had some of both over the years, but I have to say that there are so many wonderful times I have experienced that I never would have if not for my wife. I am so thankful now looking back—so much so that I may have been completely transformed in that area of my life because of my wife. We often think we are giving something up when we consider others before ourselves, but in reality life is more fulfilling when we open our hearts and allow God to use our spouses to change us.

If God wanted us to define ourselves and then stay that way, then why does it seem that almost every married couple I know is completely opposite in personality? Why do you think we are attracted to opposite personalities if we are so happy with who we are? And why is it that once we are married to that opposite personality, we try so hard to change them? The attraction is by God's design and change is the purpose. However, fights occur when we focus on changing the other instead of truly falling in love and desiring to be changed ourselves. It is true love that wants to imitate or become like the other.

So many books and studies have been done that focus on defining our differences, and I believe they are very helpful to a point. If it helps us to understand how to love the other person better, then the goal is accomplished. But if it becomes a defining and immovable structure of who you are, then you have missed the point. I have also seen these books do the opposite of what they were intended to accomplish. Instead of being helpful for understanding our spouses better, I have seen them used to create a sort of measuring stick of our own self-centered desires. I have seen some use it as a way of keeping a record of wrongs of their spouses.

My challenge to you is to embrace the differences and even the flaws between you and your spouse. Step out of your comfort zone—God wants to use you today.

Tin Man could have never survived without Dorothy. She helped him find his heart. Are you helping your spouse find his or hers?

LISTENING FOR THE DEEPER MESSAGE OF THE HEART

God is training me to hear the deeper message from my wife's heart. The message I hear is, "We're not home yet. I'm not sure I like it here. I just want to go home. I want perfection; I want heaven; I want Jesus."

I can't say I never take it personally anymore, but I can say I am learning to hear the deeper things. I am learning to hear what is not said and to answer the questions that are never asked. I can hear her now, asking, "Am I loved? Am I worth fighting for?"

The answer is a resounding YES. But am I speaking her language? Can she even hear me? I am happy to say that, with God's help, I am learning to speak "Cindy." I still need a translator sometimes; He is always there ready and willing to translate a language that only He is fluent in. Sometimes I find myself laboring over every word, struggling to make sense of things, forgetting that all I have to do is ask for a word from the Ultimate Communicator. What are my lines again?

Other times I think I am speaking eloquently and think, *I am good at this!* And then I look at her, see a confused look, and then I realize I've been speaking "James" and she has not understood a word.

As the years have gone by, my wonderful wife has learned to

be more content and to seek God to fulfill her needs. Now when I do well at loving her, she is able to enjoy my efforts instead of it being just one small effort that gets lost in a great list of expectations.

So next time you are feeling discouraged about your marriage, ask yourself if you are speaking the right language. Give yourself a break. It's not your job to make her or him feel loved; that is God's job. Your job is to love them. Find joy in that. Find joy in learning his or her language and remember there is only one translator who speaks that language fluently, so don't forget to ask for the Holy Spirit to give you just the right words to say. Your job is to love and, if you love well, the process of loving will fulfill you and give you strength that you did not know you had. It will leave you needing nothing but the author of love, Jesus.

We are made for Heaven, so it is not a surprise that we are pursuing these things. We must admit and know that we will not see perfection and we will not be completely happy until we are home in heaven with our Creator.

Once we have admitted this and agree that God has put us with the man or woman that He has for a reason, then we have to safeguard against falling back into this terrible trap that often ends in divorce.

In the next two chapters, I will begin to outline how some couples react when they notice a lack of perfection or happiness.

Chapter 7

UNDERSTANDING CONFLICT

NOBODY LIKES CONFLICT. Some people will agree with you just to avoid conflict and others will just walk away to avoid it. No matter how you handle conflict, I think you would agree that most relationship conflicts are about the way you want things to be. We find that it is easier to justify this self-focus if we can make the battle between us and someone else. However, most often the real battle is between us and God, our way versus His way. His way is to consider others better than ourselves and to put their needs before our own (Phil. 2:3). What we are talking about is sacrifice. Sacrifice is not a pleasant thought for us; by nature we have difficulty with the thought of giving something up for someone else. It makes us uncomfortable. Even though we understand Christ's example and are thankful for His sacrifice for us, it is very difficult for us to consider sacrificing our lives to give to others.

If Jesus were to stand in front of us now and ask us to do

something for Him, I can imagine that anyone who truly understands what He did for us on the cross would say, "Anything Jesus, anything at all." If you are agreeing with me, then let me ask you, Is it the thought of Jesus standing in front of you that would make you respond in such a way? Or is it just the idea of doing something directly for Jesus? What if He wanted you to do something for another human being? Do you still have the same level of enthusiasm?

Let me take the focus off you for a moment and remind you of a story in the Bible that may help to clarify this struggle.

The rich young man in Matthew 19:16-30 came up to Jesus and asked what he could do to gain eternal life. This passage is often used to warn people about the pursuit of worldly wealth and to caution them to not allow their love for money to keep them from serving God.

Today I want to dig a little deeper. I can only speculate here, but I think the man came up to Jesus excited. He was probably thinking that he would do anything for Jesus and maybe expected Jesus to ask him to do something for Him. Or, maybe he expected Jesus just to say, "Follow me," as He had said to the disciples. I think it is even possible that if Jesus asked for the man's wealth, he may have been willing to give much or all directly to Jesus. But Jesus saw his heart. He saw that the man not only loved his wealth but also was not willing to sacrifice for his fellow human beings.

It is hard for us to give up what we have for the benefit of even our loved ones, much less for strangers. Please look at this scripture from the Bible: "The King will reply, 'I tell you the truth, whatever you did for one of the least of these brothers of mine, you did for me'" (Matt. 25:40).

We must ask God to help us to have this attitude. It does not come naturally for us. We need God to transform our minds, to help us be just as willing and excited to serve others as we would be if Jesus were standing before us, asking us to do the same directly for Him. After all, He *is* asking us!

So how does this relate to conflict? Conflict often occurs when we are being asked to give something up or sacrifice for others. We become protective of our own wants and desires and sometimes our views.

How did we become so self-protective?

We start very young with a self-protection focus. God has made us with many defense mechanisms. When we are children, our parents protect us from physical harm: *Don't touch that; Walk don't run; Look both ways before you cross the street.* Protecting ourselves is obviously a learned behavior. Have you noticed, though, that even as children we did not learn until we were hurt? Although it is difficult, I believe this is what God meant for us to understand from James 1:2: "Consider it pure joy, my brothers, whenever you face trials of many kinds."

We usually stop there and say privately, "That's crazy! Who would rejoice during difficult times?" But let's read on: "...because you know that the testing of your faith develops perseverance. Perseverance must finish its work so that you may be mature and complete, not lacking anything" (James 1:3-4).

You see, the joy only comes after we have learned what God wants us to learn through the trials. The purpose of the hurt is so that we will grow and be mature.

Our parents protect us until we can protect ourselves. Then we begin to avoid difficulties to avoid being hurt. As we grow older, we avoid being hurt at all costs. In the same manner, we avoid conflict to avoid being hurt. But we are also avoiding growth.

Recently, as my wife and I have been mentoring young couples who are about to be married, we have discussed how important it is to be willing to do hard things. Doing hard things includes sacrificing your way for your mate's desires or, even better, your way for God's way. My prayer for all marriages, including my own, is that we would welcome the hard decisions as God's way of continuing His transforming work in us.

Being confident of this, that he who began a good work in you will carry it on to completion until the day of Christ Jesus. (Phil. 1:6)

Most of us try hard to avoid difficult times; however, I think we should welcome them as opportunities to grow. Too many Christian marriages end because they are not happy anymore or they are not in love anymore.

IS THERE ONE THING?

A friend of mine from my days in Wisconsin while at Bible College connected with me on Facebook and clicked over to TheAuthorOfMarriage.com. In response to one of my articles there, she wrote:

I see all your sweet, pre-marital couples online. They look so young, fresh, and happy! You must love working with them.

There have been many people in my circle who have recently divorced. These are Christian people who love God. And I know that every situation has a different story.

But here's my question. (Funny, coming from someone like me who's been married 20 years.) My marriage has had all of those "things" that break up a marriage (except infidelity—which

I consider a result, not a cause). Do you think there is one thing that keeps a marriage together?

People have commented on how lucky I am or on how much they admire that my marriage has lasted, and they ask how we do it, as if there is some secret to staying married other than just staying married!

When my kids are misbehaving and have to be punished, I've heard the famous "You don't love me" from them. I always challenge them on that, making sure they understand the difference between being mad at someone and not loving them. And if they are aware of a fight between my husband and me, I reassure them with the same explanation: "Daddy and I still love each other; we are just angry [or just disagree] on something."

So, when people ask me how we make our marriage last, my answer is that I love him. But that seems to leave an opening for falling out of love—a danger that one of those "things" could erode the love and end the marriage. So, what is it? Why do I reach a point where "I can't imagine staying with this man one more day," and yet would never walk away?

So, is hope the one thing? I know that any problem will be resolved in some fashion. If I didn't know that, would that be the end?

I've heard people say that commitment is the one thing. But that sounds so dry. Like you'd be stuck in a lifeless marriage forever just because it is the right thing to do.

Communication is another thing you are taught from premarital years on. Is it being able to discuss anything and everything with your partner that keeps a marriage cemented?

So, what do you think, James? Are there many things that destroy a marriage but one thing that holds it together? Or, are people who have been married for many years keeping a lot of balls in the air? And are they just "lucky" that one of those balls hasn't dropped? People talk about marriage being work. I don't know that I'd describe it as work, more like a lot of decisions... made with prayer, a lot of talking, and an understanding that we both want to be together.

One of my friends recently filled me in on the details of her divorce. And, despite being "experienced" at marriage, I was at a loss in trying to answer some of her questions. So, I just listened and empathized. But, this latest divorce between another Christian couple has me thinking (worrying) again about my conversation with my friend. Thought you might have some insight for me.

MY ANSWER

Thank you for your confidence in me. I do not claim to have all the answers on this subject, but as the title of my blog/ book, TheAuthorOfMarriage.com, suggests, God is the author of marriage. So, based on what I believe He says, I will try to answer the best that I can.

Is there one thing that keeps a marriage together? I think it is clear that there are different things that have been successful in keeping marriages together. As Christians, the easy answer is God. But if knowing God were the answer, then there would have to be a 100% failure in non-Christian marriages and a 100% success rate in Christian marriages, which we all know is not true.

Since your question is primarily focused on Christian couples, I will answer that first and reword your question slightly.

Is there one thing that can keep a Christian couple together?

To that question I say yes, there is one thing. Yet it may show up in the common answers like commitment, love, respect, and many more. The one thing is a willingness to change and be transformed.

If both husband and wife are committed to God and will acknowledge that the Author of marriage has a purpose for putting two people together and asking them to be one, then I believe that marriage will stay strong and last.

Most people don't ever ask what the purpose of marriage is. People get married for many reasons, including having a companion, being happy, being complete, and many more that they may not want to admit, like having someone to mow the lawn or do the dishes and cook.

I believe the answer to what can keep a couple together is also the answer to the question, "What is the purpose of marriage?"

So why does it seem that even the most godly people are not immune to divorce? I think it is again based on our willingness to change—not just changing the obvious things that we read about in the scriptures. I think the hardest things to change are the ones that we cannot find in the scriptures, like what is a wise spending choice? We do not find passages that tell us if it is OK to spend money on getting your hair done, going to the movies, which clothes to buy, how big of a TV you should have, how much money you should save, etc. What about things like parenting? We have some basics, but we are not told what grades they should get, should we push them harder, should we let them fall and pick themselves up?

Now, I am sure that somewhere in that list you said, "I know the answer to that one." But do you? And what is your answer based on? You may even say to me your answer is based on the scriptures, but I would say that your answer is based on your understanding of scriptures at this time. Now, I agree there are some things that are not grey areas and that the scriptures speak very clearly on. But what about the rest? What do you do when you think there are certain ways things should be done and your spouse disagrees with you?

So the answer to success in marriage is to be willing to change for the benefit of your spouse. But what about the things you disagree about and you have proof that your way is right? Maybe even from the scriptures?

As Christians we study the Word and sometimes with the best of intentions to know God better and love Him more. But sometimes we open God's Word to prove a point—usually about something we have already made up our minds on. If we can find support for our views, we will use it to win. This usually happens without our being aware. This is the reason that we must look again each and every day. I am sure you have read certain passages over and over and then one day you see something or understand something you did not understand before.

So with the possibility that you may not have completely understood everything about that passage you are standing on so strong, revisit your beliefs again—and do it together. The more you think you know, the harder it will be.

So my challenge is to rethink the things you think you know and have proven with scriptures. Revisit each topic.

Now, what about the things that are not clear in the scriptures? What about preferences, personality differences, or the way we grew up? These are most often the things that are the most difficult because there is no right answer. It is with these issues that we can chip away at each other. Just one difference is not a problem, but most of us have an undefined limit. This limit is influenced by our past, our upbringing, or our family tradition.

The question is, Are you willing to change these things? Some would say "Why? It is who I am." But I have to remind you that the Author of marriage says, "Consider others better than yourself." By His example we are called to sacrifice everything, including our lives, if necessary. Marriages fail because we want to keep our identities, but God wants to transform us and He wants to use our spouses to do that. Divorce is most often a resistance to the transformation.

Your question again was, "Do you think there is one thing that keeps a marriage together?"

I believe the answer is being willing to change and to sacrifice.

> Greater love has no one than this, that he lay down
> his life for his friends (John 15:13).

I'm so thankful that my friend asked me that question—What is the one thing that keeps a marriage together? Most of us will never be asked to actually give up our lives for our spouses, but giving up our wants, needs, and desires for each other is the least we can do.

I believe the reason we have trouble with sacrificing for others is our difficulty with another word: *trust*. If we really trusted God, then we would not have such difficulty with giving up our own wants and desires for Him or for others.

CHANGE YOUR THINKING

Many of us have been brought up with a concept that sounds like this: "If I don't stick up for myself, then no one else will." Or, "If it's gonna be, it's up to me."

My wife, Cindy, will share with you that she even had a coffee mug with this last concept on it at one point in her career. After trusting Christ as her Savior, she realized this was somewhat self-focused and has long since retired the mug and that philosophy.

TRUST HIM

So why don't we trust God with all of our lives? I am convinced the answer is that we do not know Him well enough. If you're like me, you've experienced both successes and failures in this area. So, allow me to leave with this challenge: let's fall on our knees, acknowledge what Jesus has done on the cross, acknowledge His sacrifice for us, and ask Him to forgive us for our self-seeking ways. Then let's turn to our spouses, children, and friends and ask them to forgive us. Big step? You bet it is! Let's determine to live each day aware of God's presence and seek Him, learn from Him, and read His love letter to us so that we can know Him better.

Chapter 8

GOING TO COURT

As you may have noticed, one of my favorite things to do at my church is to meet with married couples. I have had the privilege of meeting with some who are planning to be married and some who have been married for a while. I enjoy reminding them of what God says about marriage and helping them work through their struggles. As I have done this, I have noticed some consistencies that may help us further understand the nature of conflict.

I think we watch way too many lawyer shows, because we are getting really good at building our cases as if we are going to court. It is not very hard to find things that our spouses are doing wrong and we definitely have lists of our rights committed to memory. When things go wrong, we naturally want someone to blame, and we add that to our cases against each other even if it wasn't the other person's fault.

Many couples will agree that counseling is a good idea, but

usually the reason behind this is that one or both of them wants to find someone who will be a witness for their side, someone who will be able to get his or her spouse to see how wrong he or she is. If the person does not become aware of this tendency to be constantly building a case, it can get much worse, and the person often will extend the search for a jury. He or she will speak to friends, telling every detail, naturally leaving out any wrongdoing on his or her own part. If the friends will not see the person's side, he will sometimes even begin to distance himself from those friends and will take up new ones who agree with him (or her).

Now, this all sounds almost unbelievable, but I have seen it. The progression is ever so gradual. Many really do not see what you may see as you read this. They do not realize that they are slowly being consumed by the need to defend themselves and to defend their rights as they see them.

So what do we do about this? Whether you have found yourself in this description or you know of someone who is headed down this road, I assure you there is hope, but we must stop building cases for the world's court system. We must begin to build cases in God's court. In God's court, He is the only one who can truly meet our needs. In God's court, it is not you against your spouse. The case we must build is only for our own actions. Are we being like Christ? Do we love as He loves? Are we taking the form of a servant? Are we considering others as better than ourselves? Are we giving up things for the benefit of others? These are the things we will be judged on.

Remember the purpose of marriage is that we would be changed. I know it is really hard to break the habit of blaming our spouses. You may be thinking right now, *I'm OK with this change thing. I am willing to change, but what about her/him? My spouse needs to change, too, and if I don't let him/her know how, then he/she may not.* My friend, you will need to trust God. He does not need you to change your spouse. He does not even need your help. Stop building your case against him/her and God.

I know you may also be thinking that you need to protect yourself and defend your actions, something you probably learned when you were a child. But once again, God knows everything; He even knows the motives and thoughts behind your actions. It is His job to protect you and He loves you and wants you to let go of your defensive nature. You are not being judged in the world's court system.

Don't forget another awesome truth about God's court is that all we have to do is admit and agree with Him that we have fallen short, and He will forgive us on the spot. And if we allow Him, He will transform us and the change in us will draw our spouses to Him.

Chapter 9

PLANNING

OST OF US live our lives by planning. Some of us plan out the details of our days up to a week or month in advance. Others may not have that much forethought and detail, but there is usually at least some semblance of a plan for our days. We plan everything—or do we? Do you have a plan for today? What will you do tomorrow?

Now that I have you thinking about your plans and how well or how poorly you do in planning, let me shift slightly and get you to think about an area of your life that many do not plan well.

For a moment, let yourself off the hook and focus on how most people do in the area of planning.

Imagine for a moment that you are taking a survey. First, you enter a room full of unwed mothers. You stand there with your clipboard and ask them all by a show of hands, "How many of you planned to become mothers at this stage in your lives?" I would assume you would not see many hands. You have more questions for them, but we will pause this portion of the story much the same way as you might see in a movie with multiple story lines, and we will move to a scene in the next room where you are asking a very similar question.

In this room, there are men and women whose marriages have ended due to an affair. You ask the question, "How many of you planned to have this affair?" Once again, very few hands.

In both rooms, you ask another question, "How many of you had a plan to avoid this happening to you?" Some might have had a purpose at one time to avoid these types of things, but most do not have a detailed specific plan on how to avoid sin. And this is where I bring your planning skills back into the story. As you can see, it is absolutely essential that we have a plan to avoid sin. If we don't have a plan and if we don't stick to our plan, we will fall into sin of all kinds. So what does a plan like this look like?

We must agree that we can all be tempted in all areas of sin and we need to plan our escape. I am reminded of the story of Joseph with Potifer's wife, where she tried to seduce him. She grabbed his cloak, and he ran and left the cloak in her hands. We do not know for sure everything that was going on in Joseph's mind, but we know he was a man with a God given sex drive, So I cannot imagine him being able to resist without a detailed plan in his head. Joseph knew the way out. Do you?

Remember, we are not alone in this struggle.

> No temptation has seized you except what is common
> to man. And God is faithful; he will not let you be
> tempted beyond what you can bear. But when you are

tempted, he will also provide a way out so that you can stand up under it (1 Cor. 10:13).

Next, we must agree that we are in a battle and we must be properly armed.

I have hidden your word in my heart that I might not sin against you. (Ps. 119:11)

The best plans will include memorizing portions of God's Word that will serve as road blocks to sin. A part of your plan may include places and maybe even people you should avoid. Most of us think we are much better at resisting temptation than we really are, so your personal plan needs to be stricter than you might first think.

Finally, it is far too easy to change your plan and to think that you will not be tempted if you allow yourself to cheat on your plan. So, I recommend you find a good friend to share your plan with and ask that friend to keep you accountable.

Parents, talk about these things with your children—help them make their plans. Be very specific as you plan together. Role play some examples. Make sure they know when to just walk away from a situation. Make sure they know that God will be with them and give them strength. And most of all, remember you will need to show them that you have a plan as well.

Chapter 10

LOVE IS

I COULD NOT CLAIM the title of this book without covering the details of the "Love Chapter," First Corinthians, chapter thirteen.

Before we dive in, I want to ask you to stay with me. You may be tempted to skim or skip part of this if you have heard lots of teaching from this chapter. I want you to remember that God's Word is alive, and it will benefit you to look again at this section more deeply.

God wants us to love our spouses as He loves us. I know this may sound overwhelming, but He will do the work in us if we will let Him.

My command is this: Love each other as I have loved you. Greater love has no one than this, that he lay down his life for his friends. (John 15:12-13)

A good friend of mine has recently developed a church class based on the "Love Chapter." The following has been inspired in part by his teachings, and, if he ever publishes his teachings, I will update our website to include his material.

First, I want you to imagine yourself in the Garden of Eden. Imagine what it must have been like. No pain, no fear, no sin, no stress, and, in contrast, this place was the most fun, most peaceful, intriguing, and fascinating place of all time. It was better than any movie or fairy tale you have ever heard. There was adventure, romance, and a heavenly perfection that would give you a small glimpse into what heaven will be like.

You explore every day and find new plants and animals that you have never seen before, and by far the best thing about it all is that you are not alone. You have daily conversations directly with your Creator who loves you and has all the time in the world to just talk about the wonders of the world He has created. He loves you so much that He also gave you a companion, and not just someone like you but someone who is very different. He calls her *woman* because she was created specifically for you. She is beautiful beyond words, and you cannot believe how much God loves you to give such an amazing creature as a mate. Her beauty is deeper than the obvious physical features; you love to talk to her and are intrigued at the differences in the way you think. You begin right away trying to figure her out as this seems to be your place in this world.

You are not alone! It is different from the relationships you have with the other creatures here in the garden. Not only is she more beautiful than all the rest, but also she is the only one you can talk to. You enjoy this and take lots of walks around the garden. Occasionally on your walks, you run into the outer walls of the garden. You often wonder what is on the other side.

However, you can't imagine anything better than being here safe within the garden walls.

You live this way for some time and never get bored until the day that you make that choice. Exercising your free will, you decide you want more.

As you imagine all of this, I want you to keep in mind how safe and protected you felt as you imagined being Adam. Although he was expelled from the garden because of his sin, I am sure he often thought of the garden after leaving. The bad news is that we can never return to the garden. The good news is that heaven will be exponentially better than the garden, and, even though we cannot return to the Garden of Eden, we can build a metaphorical garden wall around ourselves, a place that is safe and peaceful—and a place where our focus is completely devoted to building a godly marriage. We must have God's help to build this wall. The wall of love includes many building blocks. With God's help, we can build up the walls to the garden every day. The difference with this wall is that there are many forces outside of these walls that will try to break in and damage what we have built. But if we work at it every day and ask God to help us repair and protect our wall, we can truly experience the love God intended.

The blocks of love belong on the wall surrounding a husband and wife. We must not allow any walls to be built between us. It is a daily process to tear down the walls between us and to put the blocks back on the garden wall.

The walls of love that protect us and make up the garden wall include blocks representing each of the "Love is" and "Love does" statements in God's definition of love found in the book of First Corinthians, chapter thirteen.

Love is patient, love is kind. It does not envy, it does not boast, it is not proud. It is not rude, it is not self-seeking, it is not easily angered, it keeps no record of wrongs. Love does not delight in evil but rejoices with the truth. It always protects, always trusts, always hopes, always perseveres. Love never fails. (1 Cor. 13:4-8a)

Now I would like to cover each of these ingredients of love as defined by The Author of Marriage.

BE PATIENT

Love is patient. The first block is patience. Love is patient. What does it really look like if we are patient? Patience seems to always involve waiting. But waiting for what? It is obvious that if we wrongly focus on the changes that we feel our spouses need to make, then being patient may lead to the question, "How long?" which actually shows that we are not patient. Not being patient might be an indication that we do not trust God—which would also be an indication that we do not know God or that we do not believe He is who He says He is. It is obvious that we must have God's help to be patient and in turn to love the way He wants us to. However, we still must exercise our free will and be patient.

BE KIND

Love is kind. Being kind seems so easy. Isn't this also a choice? Our second building block in the garden is kindness. There are many reasons why we are not always kind. Sometimes it is because we have been hurt and react in an unloving and unkind way. It definitely takes work to be kind. But again, we are not alone and we cannot build the wall without God's help. God's example shows us that love and love's kindness should be unconditional. We should be kind in word and in deed. It is easier to be kind when your spouse has been kind first. I encourage you to be the first.

A friend of mine told me something once that I am not sure of the original source, but the statement has helped me many times in my marriage. That statement is, "The first one to the cross wins!" This is a mental process that acknowledges the sacrifice of Christ on the cross and agrees that we are not perfect, that we need to be forgiven, and on that foundation we can keep building. We need to compete with our spouses when it comes to being kind as well as all of the other elements of love. We have at times made this fun, and it has produced laughter, which is healing.

Let me say, just be kind and you might be surprised about how easily your issues will fade away.

> Above all, love each other deeply, because love covers
> over a multitude of sins. (1 Pet. 4:8)

As I mentioned, we should choose to be kind with our words even when our spouses have not been kind. We should not retaliate as seen in First Peter: "Don't repay evil for evil. Don't retaliate with insults when people insult you. Instead, pay them back with a blessing. That is what God has called you to do, and he will bless you for it" (1 Pet. 3:9, NLT).

Consider also this verse: "*Be kind* and compassionate to one another, forgiving each other, just as in Christ God forgave you" (Eph. 4:32, emphasis added). As you can see in this verse, the foundation of kindness is forgiveness. We are called to forgive as Christ forgave us.

> Therefore, as God's chosen people, holy and dearly loved, clothe yourselves with compassion, kindness, humility, gentleness and patience. (Col. 3:12)

There it is—right there in God's Word. Put on kindness like you put on your clothes in the morning. Memorize it. I'm going to!

> Bear with each other and forgive whatever grievances you may have against one another. Forgive as the Lord forgave you. (Col. 3:13)

It doesn't matter if you have forgiven your spouse over and over again, and it also does not matter if he or she even acknowledges these things or even asks for your forgiveness.

> And over all these virtues put on love, which binds them all together in perfect unity. (Col. 3:14)

Love binds all of those virtues together, meaning they are all a part of love as defined by *God*.

BE CONTENT

Love does not envy. Being content is a command from God.

> Keep your lives free from the love of money and *be content* with what you have, because God has said,

"Never will I leave you; never will I forsake you." (Heb. 13:5, emphasis added)

It is not a suggestion. God wants us to acknowledge Him as our provider, and in doing so He wants us to admit that He has given us *all* we need. Not just part of what we need.

His divine power has given us everything we need for life and godliness through our knowledge of him who called us by his own glory and goodness. (2 Pet. 1:3)

"His divine power" indicates that He knows everything, including what we need and what we want. And it is with this same power that He commands us to be content.

Being content with what we have most definitely includes being content with the spouses that He has given us. Discontentment is one of the core reasons for many divorces. One or both people say, "I deserve better" and justify their actions to leave.

If we are not content with our marriages, then we are not trusting God, and we do not believe that He really knows what we need.

Once again, if the purpose of marriage is to change me, then the woman God gave me is part of that plan, and He has written contentment into the very definition of love.

Every time we complain, we are questioning God and refusing to be content.

If we are not content with the spouses God has given, we are not trusting God, and we are elevating our own worth above the other. There is that pride again—the killer of love as God designed it.

Be Modest

Love does not boast. True love will lift up others, not ourselves. Boasting seems to be an obvious one; however, it is closely tied to the previous ingredient of contentment. If you are not content, you will have the tendency to boast about yourself and by doing so put the other down.

> Do nothing out of selfish ambition or vain conceit, but in humility consider others better than yourselves. (Phil. 2: 3)

Being critical and judgmental is also a form of boasting.

Be Humble

It is not proud. Being proud is almost synonymous with being human and is likely the foundational reason why we find it so hard to love as described here. It is impossible for us to really love like this without allowing God's Holy Spirit to take over. We must die to ourselves so that Christ may reign in us.

> I have been crucified with Christ and I no longer live, but Christ lives in me. The life I live in the body, I live by faith in the Son of God, who loved me and gave himself for me. (Gal. 2:20)

BE CONSIDERATE

Love is not rude. Being considerate of the other person is more than just being kind or patient. Rudeness is to intentionally tear someone else down. We can be rude with our words and this can occur privately as well as in public. Usually the reason is we are hurt and want to hurt the person back. Our pride is what causes rudeness.

We can also be rude with our silence. To hold back kindness and not say what we should say is also rude. Some will say, "If I say something, I am sure it will be wrong, so I just won't say anything at all." If you have ever said this, I challenge you to ask God to change your heart, ask Him to give you the right words to say, and then say them. It does not have to be eloquent, but complete silence can be rude.

How can we be considerate? Simply think of our spouses first. Knowing them is a necessary part of being considerate. For example, if you know your spouse needs to hear your positive words of encouragement, then you should be considerate and provide these wholesome and uplifting comments with a consistent regularity. Or if your spouse feels loved when you accomplish tasks for him or her, then you should find every opportunity to serve your spouse in this way.

BE SELFLESS

Love is not self-seeking. Again, this one is tied so closely to pride. It is pride that causes us to think about ourselves first. Pride and self-seeking produce arguments or fights, fueling our desire to fight for our own way. Ask yourself—do I always try to get other people to see things the way I see them?

In fact, that is the reason I am writing this book—I want you to see what I see! But wait! God in me does not want that. He wants you to see His way. I pray that He is able to use me and my words here to draw you closer to Him.

Seeking God's best for your spouse is the opposite of being self-seeking. Again, it is only by God's divine intervention that you will be able to think of your spouse first. Ask Him daily to help you. If you stay connected to God, He will love your spouse through you.

BE CALM

Love is not easily angered. Being calm is easier if we really believe that God is in control. I think we sometimes question this because we do not understand why God allows certain things. We must trust Him and believe that He sees everything, and nothing ever comes as a surprise to Him. There is a purpose for everything that He allows to happen.

Anger usually starts with not getting our way. It is also common to feel anger when we have been hurt.

> A gentle answer turns away wrath, but a harsh word
> stirs up anger. (Prov. 15:1)

Sometimes we are hurt because someone has challenged our thinking or said things that were unkind. We cannot justify our anger just because our spouses do not love us as described here.

Let me point out that the verse in First Corinthians, chapter thirteen, does not say we should never be angry. It only says we should not be easily angered. It is true that some types of anger are OK—for example, being angry at sin. God makes it clear there is a fine line here.

> In your anger do not sin: Do not let the sun go down while you are still angry. (Eph. 4:26)

It seems here that allowing your anger to control you is sin.

BE FORGIVING

Love keeps no record of wrongs. We're not allowed to keep score. Forgiving someone like God forgives us includes asking God to help us forget. It is so easy to store up ammunition for your next fight and commit to memory the things your spouse has done, but this is not love. I have covered forgiveness in chapter three, so I will not repeat all of those things here. I do want to remind us once again that forgiveness is the foundation for healing in a marriage.

BE UPLIFTING

Love does not delight in evil. When I got to this one, I said, "Really? Who actually delights in evil?" And then I thought of the verse earlier from First Peter 3:9 which says, "Do not repay evil with evil."

By nature we are so reactive. When someone does us wrong, we react and retaliate. The interesting thing is that we justify this in our minds and do not even call it what it is. I think if we are truthful, we often secretly enjoy hurting people who have hurt us. Ouch! That was hard to say. But let's be real here. Look what the Bible says:

The heart is deceitful above all things, and desperately wicked: who can know it? (Jer. 17:9, KJV)

We must see our own need to change so that we are able to love our spouses the way God intended.

BE TRUTHFUL

Love rejoices with the truth. Before I talk about being truthful to each other, I want to look at what Jesus said about himself: "Jesus answered, 'I am the way and the truth and the life. No one comes to the Father except through me'" (John 14:6).

To rejoice with the truth is to rejoice in the life, death, and resurrection of Jesus. This is another reminder that we should be following Jesus' example of love when loving our spouses. No matter what you're going through, no matter how bad your marital issues are, one thing is always true—the Truth will set you free.

To the Jews who had believed Him, Jesus said, "If you hold to my teaching, you are really my disciples. Then you will know the truth, and *the truth will set you free.* (John 8:31-33, emphasis added)

Now, to the topic of being truthful to your spouse. Obviously this is a very important part of building trust between you. Love always tells the truth; however, this does not mean that we must tell them everything.

Now, I am sure I am going to get a lot of questions or people disagreeing with me on this, but try to understand the heart of what I am saying. A first and obvious example would be this: You see your wife while she is getting ready to go out one evening, and you notice that she has put on a few pounds. If sharing everything is the same as being truthful, then you would have to volunteer your thoughts by saying, "Wow, you're getting fat!" Obviously, this would not be a loving thing to say. So I hope you are with me so far.

Now, what if she were to come out and ask if she looked fat in the outfit she was wearing? If you truthfully think she does look fat in that outfit then anything but the absolute truth of "yes" would be a lie, right? Now, I am not sure, but I suppose it might be possible for some women to actually want to hear the truth. But most are actually asking a different question. They already know the answer to the question they are asking, and even if you say "no," they will likely not believe you or choose to believe their own opinion. The real question is, "Am I still beautiful? Are you still attracted to me? Do you still see my loveliness, in spite of the fact that I have gained some weight?"

I hope you are still with me on this because it is very important that we understand this fine line. The line between truthfulness and protecting is difficult to determine. It is going to be different for each couple. In order to rightly define this line, you will have to really know your spouse. Some may decide they should protect their spouses from the truth of financial difficulties and actually agree with each other on these things. But be careful—make sure you don't use this as a justification to hide things from each other without permission.

BE PROTECTIVE

Love always protects. Protecting each other can be done in a variety of ways, one of which I have already alluded to. If our motives are godly, we may sometimes protect each other by withholding hurtful truths. This would be protecting them emotionally.

Another way we can protect our spouses is to be wise with

money, spending, etc. A good spending plan and good communication and guidelines that are mutually agreed upon can be very helpful in protecting your financial household. Don't hesitate to seek professional help for budgeting as well as financial planning advice. I know of an excellent financial planner, if you don't already have one. Go to CindyPrice.com and ask my wife for an appointment!

BE TRUSTING

Love always trusts. Love believes the best of each other. Trust is a choice. If we determine our spouses' trustworthiness by their past mistakes, then we are not loving them as Christ loves and forgives us. In order to trust them, it requires that we forgive them; if we forgive them as God forgives us, then we will not use those things against them.

It is our job to build their trust in us, making it easier for them to trust us. The problem is that we are afraid to trust because we might get hurt. They might not be worthy of our trust. If we love them and trust them, we think they will abuse that trust. But the truth is that the only way we can help our spouses is to love and trust them unconditionally and have faith in God. We must not forget this is God's way of loving. If we can love like this, then His love can do its job. We have to believe there is something magical about loving His way; it is healing, forgiving, trusting, and, yes, gently convicting. Deep down we know we do not deserve to be loved like this, and that is what often initiates the change in us.

BE HOPEFUL

Love always hopes. Our hope needs to be in the Lord first. We have hope because He loves us and has a perfect plan for our lives.

But how do we love our spouses with hope? I think part of hope is believing that God is in control of them. It is a choice to have hope in their potential, to believe they can do great things. Hope is encouraging. I have written a lot about encouraging each other—it is our job to cheer them on to greatness.

Another way we can love with hope is to have an uplifting spirit—to believe that the circumstances of our lives will get better and that God will use even the things we perceive as bad for His glory. Again, this is a choice and it is physically seen. Choosing to have hope can literally change your outward appearance.

BE PERSEVERING

Love always perseveres. If we have hope, we will also choose to persevere. We will keep climbing the mountain of love even when we are discouraged. Love never gives up. This is the love we dream of! The best movies and stories we have heard from childhood are the ones where the prince never quit. He went after her against all obstacles and opposition! The heroes and heroines that make the best movies are the ones who never gave up; they kept pushing themselves beyond what some even thought possible. This is perseverance.

I have great news for you today. If you have made a decision to trust Christ as your Savior, then you, too, can be a hero! Really! You can be the greatest hero that ever lived. Why do I say this with such confidence? Because *The Hero*, the one who created all the heroes who have ever lived, lives in you. The only limit is your faith.

And by the way—your husband or wife deserves to be married to a hero.

Love Never Fails

Failure is not an option! Sounds like a line I have heard in many movies. It is a choice to love this way, but the moment we fail to be patient, kind...at that moment we have ceased to love.

The best part of all of this is that this last statement is the guarantee. I am not talking about a limited guarantee. I am talking about a guarantee that is secured by the Creator of the world. The guarantee is that if we love consistently and depend on God to help us love the way He does, then we will win.

Impossible, you say? Yes it is, but with God all things are possible.

Jesus looked at them and said, "With man this is impossible, but with God all things are possible." (Matt. 19:26)

How? It isn't possible to be that godly. True, it is a process and we will never completely arrive until we reach heaven, but if we seek first the Kingdom of God each and every day, He will help us to take down the walls separating us from our spouses, and then He will help us to put those sections of the walls back on our own personal garden walls. If we stay connected to Him, He will help that wall stay in place. Remember, He is the vine and that vine is growing on the wall. As time goes by, we will produce fruit.

When we love each other as God intended, the imaginary wall of love is completely intact and surrounding us. Again, I want you to acknowledge before God that all of this is impossible without Him. You cannot even begin to love this way without being filled to overflowing with God's love for you. It is only when we confess our sin that God will fill us with His Holy Spirit. If we allow Him to, He will guide and direct us in word and in deed.

As seen earlier in John 15:5, God says He is the vine and we are the branches. The vine is the only *One* who can hold the garden wall together, but He chooses to use us (the branches), and from the branches the possibility of bearing fruit is dependent on staying connected to the Vine. And while we are connected, we will produce the fruit of the Spirit.

> But the fruit of the Spirit is love, joy, peace, patience, kindness, goodness, faithfulness, gentleness and self-control. Against such things there is no law. (Gal. 5:22-23)

Without the fruit of the Spirit we cannot love the way God loves.

Now that we have covered some foundational truths, I want to cover some gender-targeted thoughts that may be helpful to you.

LOVING YOUR HUSBAND

Before I get started, I have to answer your question. *What about loving your wife?* Don't worry; that topic will be next. Although this section will focus on women loving their husbands, much of it can also be applied to husbands loving their wives.

One of the hardest times for a woman to encourage

her husband is when she feels like her needs are not being met. Some women will make sure their husbands know they are not measuring up. This will, in most cases, make things even worse. One of my favorite statements about men comes from a great book called *Wild at Heart,* by John Eldredge.*

The statement is, "Every man has a question. Do I have what it takes?" The answer he fears is, "No." During times of difficulty with his job, his relationship with his wife or kids, this fear may be greater. He may not show it, but it is there. So what can a woman do to help him out of a difficult time? You have to love him the way he needs to be loved. Do you know what that is? In his book, *The Five Love Languages,* Gary Chapman encourages wives to ask themselves and their husbands what makes them feel loved:

Does he feel loved when you say encouraging things to him?

Does he feel loved when you are affectionate and intimate with him?

Does he feel loved when you spend time with him?

Does he feel loved when you do things for him?

Or does he feel loved when you give him gifts?**

If you can't answer which one of those is the most important, then ask him, "When was the last time you felt loved by me?" His answer will tell you what his most important love language is.

Usually when our needs are not being met, we immediately let our spouses know. What if we reach out and, forgetting our own needs, we first find out if their needs are being met?

---

* Eldredge. *Wild at Heart.*
** Chapman. *The Five Love Languages.*

An illustration I like is that of a road trip. We start out on a trip across country, pick our favorite destination, and an hour into the trip I notice that the fuel gauge is on empty. Instead of stopping, I fly by a gas station, and another, and finally my car comes to a sputtering halt. I get out of the car and start yelling at it, kicking the tires and explaining how important it is that we get where we are going. None of this helps. It would not do any good to put water, diesel fuel, or straight oil in the gas tank. If my car takes gas, I must put gas in the tank.

This all seems kind of silly, but it is often how we treat our spouses. We must take the necessary time to find out what kind of fuel our spouses need and regularly fill them up with our love. When we do this, it is more likely that we will get the fuel we need.

So prepare well for the road trip and have fun. Fun? Yes, marriage is supposed to be fun.

Now let me expound on the importance of understanding your spouse's love language. I will use a real life illustration here. As I write this, I am challenged myself. I know that, even if no one ever reads this, God has at least used the process of writing about marriage to make me a better man. If you knew me personally, you might be surprised to hear of my struggles. As I have worked on this book, I have often wondered, *Why? Why am I writing this?* Certainly not because I feel I am good at writing—even my wife says that she feels I am much better in person. I have had a few friends say they like what they read, but it does not seem to be enough. I share this with you because I do not want you to ever feel like you are alone in your struggle with confidence. Even if you have not heard them say it out loud, I can guarantee that everyone you have ever respected, including pastors, authors, community leaders, and even presidents who have held the highest position in our land have problems with confidence. Perhaps they are really good at hiding it, but they all give in to fear at certain times of their lives.

So I share all of this to make you feel better if you doubt your abilities, but I also share it to make me feel better. After all, I am in good company when I doubt myself!

Finally, I want to help you to see the power of your encouragement on your spouse. Even though I have had many friends encourage me, it is not enough. The only person I really want to impress is my wife. If she were to say, "You are a really good writer. You should really focus on finishing this book," that would be all I would need. Just in case you think poorly of my wife, let me explain that she has said very positive things about me and my work. She does encourage me the best she knows how. You see, she speaks a different language. She does not use the same words I do. If she says, "That's good," after reading something I have written, I need to hear, "That is amazing!" or "That is really good, excellent, incredible!" My interpretation of "That's good" is "Nothing to write home about" or "It's just OK." Even her statement of "You're much better in person" means to me "Don't quit your day job; you're really not very good at this."

Obviously one of my primary love languages is "Words of Affirmation." I am not sure what causes this great need. I remember my parents being very encouraging, so it is not because I have been lacking in encouragement.

Now let me be clear that this is how I feel loved. When my wife goes out of her way to compliment me, I feel loved. The key for me and anyone else who also feels loved by affirming words is to remember that God says you are fearfully and wonderfully made. These are words of encouragement that can be found in God's Word. We need to be careful not to place too much significance in our spouses' abilities to communicate in just the right way to make us feel loved. The key is that everyone needs to learn his or her spouse's love language and speak it with fluency.

LOVING YOUR WIFE

If you have not already guessed, one of my favorite authors is John Eldredge. I have had the privilege of leading men at my church in a study of his book *Wild at Heart*. In the study, we show a video of the author and four of his friends who have gone to a ranch to explore what it means to be "wild at heart." He states in his book that every man longs for a battle to fight, an adventure to live, and a beauty to rescue. He shares with men that every man has one question: "Do I have what it takes?" And every woman asks, "Am I lovely?"

One of the last sessions in the video series after a few days of just the men talking and living in the adventure, they invite their wives to join them at this ranch. At one point, John asks the women, "What does a woman want from her husband?" One of the wives says, "To be pursued, to be seen, to be pursued until I am seen." Wow, that's deep. But that is the point—a woman wants to be seen as deep, fascinating, and worth pursuing.

I don't know how many times I have heard men say things like, "Who can understand a woman? Just when you think you understand her, she changes." I have seen men become frustrated with trying to figure out their wives. Men want to come up with a definition of their wives that will help them manage. They are looking for a system. But a system will never work.

Men, your wives do not want you to figure them out. They

want you to pursue the depths of their hearts each and every day and then they want you to start all over again tomorrow. They want to remain somewhat mysterious, to keep your interest.

There are many books written about understanding a woman or understanding the differences between men and women. What is most interesting is that many of these books are written by men. Some men have just given up and others seem to want to define a woman in an attempt to create a system they can follow. It is my belief that both of these pursuits are wrong.

There are so many similarities in our relationship with God and our relationship with our wives. God wants to have a relationship with us. It is more than just learning the rules and following them. He wants us to endlessly pursue understanding Him and knowing Him. In the same way, His design of the woman is such that we can pursue understanding her for the rest of our lives and will just begin to scratch the surface of true understanding. Intimacy is only obtained by knowing each other. I don't think it is a mistake that the King James Version of the Bible often uses the word *know* to describe sexual intimacy.

> And *Adam knew* Eve his wife; and she conceived, and bare Cain, and said, I have gotten a man from the Lord. (Gen. 4:1 KJV)

Although it is the desire of most women to be known, it is also true that they never want us to say or think we know them with any finality. I think most women have this secret fear: that her husband will one day stop pursuing her because he thinks he has figured her out. No woman wants to hear the words "You always" or "You never" because this is an indication that the one saying these words thinks he is finished pursuing and has completed the book titled *I Know Everything There is to Know About my Wife*. It is also true that we all can change. In fact, being willing to change is the foundational principle of this book. So, if our wives are doing their parts to be changed every day by the transforming work of the Holy Spirit, then as soon as we learn something about them, that characteristic may change by tomorrow—and we should always allow for that change. I have observed some couples who have been married for many years become stagnant in their marriages because either one or both are no longer willing to change. But I have also seen some people who genuinely want to change, but their spouses seem to sort of trap them where they are by using defining and absolute comments. We must not judge the attempts of our wives to change, no matter how long they have possessed certain characteristics or behaviors. Below is a personal prayer of mine that may help you to not be a hindrance to your wife's spiritual journey.

Lord, help me to give my wife the freedom to change without my criticism or comments of unbelief. Help me to have faith in your ability to change her to be more like you. And at the same time, help me to not focus on what change I think should occur in her. Help me to be constantly reminded of the fact that I am only responsible for change in myself, and help me to trust you and your plan for her spiritual growth. Help me to be gracious and forgiving, and please give me a dose of your ability to forget what was and to start new today, giving her a clean slate. And finally, Lord God, I know you know this, but it will help me to say it now: I love you and ask you now to forgive me for thinking more highly of myself than I ought to. Forgive me for anything I have done or said that has hindered what you are trying to do in my wife. Help me to be a good example to her and to my children. Thank you for giving me the gift of communication. I now ask you to help me to know when to lead in silence and when to speak out. This is my prayer for today—that you will be glorified by all that I do and say. Amen

You must give your wife the freedom to change without judging and keeping your record of past wrongs—our judgments will serve as a barrier to grace.

As we further explore complete understanding of our wives, I encourage you to be sensitive to the times you choose to pursue her. You should develop a good sense of your wife's current mood.

When your wife seems to be in a bad mood, sometimes she may want to be left alone, but other times she may want you to find out why. You may say, "I can't read minds." You don't need to; you just need to know her. Don't try to fix her, judge her, or tell her to snap out of it. Say something like, "Sounds like you have had a bad day; would you like to talk about it? Is there anything I can do?"

Chapter 11

LOVE SERVES

WE HAVE COVERED the definition of *love* in the previous chapter, but knowing and understanding the definition of *love* is the first step. Love requires action. It is in the serving that we find and begin to understand the true definition of *love*.

Our minds are by far our biggest battlefield, as explained by Joyce Meyer in *Battlefield of the Mind*.* The struggles are daily and sometimes even more frequent. We must have God's help to win these battles—which means we need to keep a very short list and stay connected all day long.

I have often shared that we need to ask God to change our hearts and the actions will follow, which is very true. But it is just as true that sometimes we need to just do what God says, even if we don't feel like it. We know the right things to do,

---

* Meyer. *Battlefield of the Mind.*

many of them you probably knew even before beginning this journey with me. But I also hope you have learned some new things also.

In either case, my question is, Did you really learn these things? If you truly learned something and it is more than just head knowledge, then you will need to practice. Practice really does make perfect, or at least it is part of the perfecting of our faith. We hear, we process, we commit to memory, and the final step is that we act on what we have learned. "Repeat as necessary" is something we can read on the bottles of many products we buy at the drug store. The learning process does not necessarily end once you have successfully acted on what you have learned. The next time you are challenged with the same situation, it should be a little easier than the first time, but this depends on so many things. Did you relax after doing it right the first time? Did you really commit the new truth to memory? Do you still believe it is true? You may need to repeat some or all of the steps to changing, not just your mind but your actions as well.

Serving Together

One of the best ways to practice your ministry to your spouse is to practice together by ministering to others who are in need. Ministering to others individually and together is a wonderful, natural, and effective way to take this truth, turn it into action, and then, by repeating that action, turning it into a habit.

Just the other day, while sitting with my men's Bible study group, I was sharing with them some of these truths. I was talking about some of the struggles we still had after sixteen years of being married, and one of the topics was the occasional disagreement about how we spend money. I am sure that is not a surprise to you as most couples struggle with these issues at some point in their marriages. Anyhow, I was sharing with them how my wife worries about money. I have tried to protect her heart by handling our finances so that she does not need to see each dollar being spent. This has always been a difficulty for her and I have done the best I can over the years to protect her from the stress she feels when she sees the money leave our accounts and go to someone else. Some of you are thinking this is unusual for a woman to be that concerned about these things. It typically seems to be more of a difficulty for men. But as a financial planner, my wife works with people all day helping them to save for their futures. So for her, every dollar leaving is a dollar not saved.

As I was sharing these things with the men in my group, I realized that my original goal to protect her was very good, but complete protection from the details of our finances has at times caused her to think our financial situation is worse than it really is. I realized and shared with the guys that there was probably a good compromise. If I did a better job preparing a report of our budget versus actual spending, she would most likely be encouraged to see that we often come under budget.

However, there is a personal struggle I sometimes have. I want her to trust me. I am embarrassed even now to say that I unconsciously test her trust in me. I think I take her fear as a lack of faith in me. You see, trust and respect are two of the most sought-after measures of a man's sense of self worth. So because of my own questions of self worth, I test her by not sharing with her the things she needs to know. We often need to revisit these areas of our lives and check in to see—Have her needs changed?

Have the circumstances of life changed? After taking stock of what you have learned again, discuss together what needs to change to accommodate each other's updated needs.

Serving others together as a couple is so effective. Every time my wife and I teach a class, mentor a new couple, or take a call from someone in crisis, we reinforce the things we know. And every time we say these things to someone, they sink in a little deeper, and at some point they begin to actually change who we are. Sound a little like brainwashing? It is. Only when we use God's Word as our text, it is good. We cannot help but be affected by verbally sharing with other couples how God has helped us in the past. The more often we tell the good stories, the more solidified they become in our minds. As I wrote earlier, some of those things become road blocks keeping us from traveling the road of destruction.

Some people serve side by side all day long, like my mother and father who served God together for almost forty years in Venezuela. I am not sure how they did that. My wife and I have often chuckled about this, thinking there is no way we could do that. I mean, most days they were less than one hundred yards from each other all day long. I am so in awe of them!

Cindy and I are very effective while serving together for several hours at a time, but we know our limits. It's not that we can't work together for longer periods of time, but if we give everything we have in serving someone, after a few hours or so we need time to recharge.

Just as strongly as I suggest that you serve together, I also want you to always remember that serving needs to begin at home. I have seen some people spend so much time serving at church that they allow their home lives to suffer.

I personally had a revelation about serving on a recent trip we took. We were staying with a friend, and after dinner I found myself trying to be a good guest. I washed dishes and cleaned like I had not done in years. I even finished by wiping down the sinks and polishing the faucet handles. I was really enjoying serving. And then it hit me. I do not clean like that at home. I was a little embarrassed as I thought about this. Why? The only reason I could think of was that I was a guest. Then I heard God's message to me. We should serve at home as if we are guests. It didn't take long for me to realize that we really are guests in our own homes. If God is our provider, and if He owns everything, then my house is not really mine. God has entrusted me with a home, a wife, and children. If I am to be a good steward of what He has given me, then I need to serve at home as if I am a guest.

I want to encourage you to step back and take a good long look at why you do what you do every day. Whether you and your spouse are serving God together or simply serving each other, take a good look at why you're doing what you do every day and how that impacts you, your marriage, your family, and the world around you.

Are You Building Castles?

Some time ago, my family and I were at the beach. It was a beautiful day and my son Matt (age ten) and his sister Heather (age six) were playing in the sand. I was sitting in a beach chair, trying to read a book I had brought with me. Several times while I was reading, one of the children asked if I would come play. I don't remember even which one it was, because I was trying hard to concentrate on what I was reading. When I finally realized

I had read the same paragraph several times and still did not know what I had read, I gave in and put down my book.

As I sat down in the sand, I noticed that, unlike many children who play on the beach, they were not building castles. Instead, they were focused on digging. I quickly adjusted and began helping them. The frustration of not being able to read my book quickly faded away as I became committed to digging deeper (not realizing at the time the significance). We dug several large holes and then began digging trenches that filled with water every time the waves came in. As the holes filled in, we noticed little creatures swimming in the pools of water. Every time we dug out a handful of sand, they would scurry across the bottom of the pool and then disappear into the sand. No matter how deep we dug, they seemed to want to go deeper! And then it hit me. These little guys might just have something! There is treasure below the surface. Sometimes it is hard to find, but it is there.

It is very easy for us to lose focus of what is really important in life. The majority of our days are filled with building castles. It is obvious that we need money to live, but when is it enough? If we really believe what we learn from Crown Financial Ministries and all the wonderful supporting scripture, we would have to agree that it all belongs to our Creator, and He has entrusted us with the proper management of what He has given us.* What would it look like if we were to only take what we need from our income to live and give the rest back to Him?

The other thing I was reminded of is that the real treasure

---

* For more information about Crown Financial Ministries, visit www. crown.org.

is just below the surface. Dig a little deeper; you will find it. Interpret this how you may, but what comes to mind is my relationship with my wife, my children, and all of you. So remember, the purpose for our lives is not to build castles, but rather to dig for treasures of God's Word, our relationship with Him, and the relationships He has given us.

Chapter 12

COMMUNICATION

COMMUNICATION—THIS IS THE big one, isn't it? Some people are naturally good communicators, and others dread every conversation. One of the reasons some people don't like to talk is they don't think they are any good at communicating. They feel it does not work or produce the results they would like. This is called manipulation and can only be resolved by understanding that the purpose of communication is to understand each other, not to change each other.

If you find it difficult to communicate, I suggest you start by writing your thoughts back and forth. Sometimes verbal communication can be frustrating when you can't seem to complete a thought before being interrupted. It is also helpful for the person receiving the written word. They can read the same words several times if needed to ensure their complete understanding of the other.

Some people mistakenly think they are not being understood

because their spouses do not do what they want. For example, my wife feels loved when I do things for her, so when I don't do exactly what she wants, she assumes that I don't love her. It is hard for her to draw the line between her desire to feel love and the common struggle to want to control all of her surroundings. I am sure you have heard the common statement, "If you cared about me, you would…" You may assume that the person saying this is wrong, but it also is evidence that the person he or she is addressing may not be doing enough things out of free will to show love.

I Care—Or I Want?

Most communication problems occur because we tend to see communication as a way of getting what we want! If we do not trust that God can change our spouses without our help, then it is likely we will use communication as a way to attempt to change them. However, the true purpose of communication is supposed to be about understanding and knowing each other, not changing each other.

Some people avoid talking altogether. They wrongly think they are not good at communicating, so they just stop. What they don't realize is that even if they don't talk, they are still communicating very strongly about what they want. Their lack of willingness to talk is also communicating that if they can't make their spouses change or see things their way, then they don't want to talk.

It has been helpful for my wife and me to take time to spend together and have a date night. Also, we try to make time every evening for shorter conversations. When we miss a few opportunities, it often causes more stressful conversations when we do get a chance to talk. If we wait until we have to communicate, then it often seems negative and is not enjoyable.

My wife has mentioned on a few occasions that she feels I always win when we communicate, which is one reason she does not like to talk. It is obvious that I am not as good a communicator as I think I am, and it is also obvious that I can sometimes use my skill in a less-than-glorifying way. But why do we feel we have to win in communication? Neither of us should be losing. If we learn something from the conversation, then we both win. And if we trust God and allow Him to change us through every conversation, then He wins and so do we.

ARGUMENTS

Arguments—this is the number one reason why people give up on trying to communicate with their spouses. It's hard to continue to talk when the last few times you've attempted a conversation, an argument ensued. However, if you use the skills I have outlined here, and if you take turns speaking, you will have fewer arguments, and communicating will slowly become less intimidating, more effective, and even enjoyable.

One thing I love to do is communicate with married or about-to-be-married couples. I speak at men's meetings, marriage seminars, and retreats, but my favorite spot to talk is on my blog at www.TheAuthorofMarriage.com. I hope you'll join me there this week!

My wife and I teach a pre-married group in our church that meets every eight weeks. All the couples faithfully attended the class except one woman who was there without her fiancé because he was serving our country in Iraq. I connected with her husband on Facebook so he wouldn't feel left out of the pre-married counseling we do in the group sessions. I wanted to share one particular online encounter where the husband shared his thoughts with me concerning arguments that were going on between him and his wife. He's graciously given me his permission to share his thoughts and questions followed by my responses to him online.

To James:

It's hard to say I look forward to an argument, but I wish I could have talked to you before to help me wrap my mind around the bigger picture when my wife and I weren't seeing eye-to-eye. There are many distractions here (in another culture/nation) and it has been too easy for me to stray.

I'm grateful for this opportunity to take this course—obstacles and all. Thank you for all you have done and continue to do. —R

To R:

Thanks for the reply. Communication is hard when you can sit across the table and discuss things, so I can imagine how much harder it is to communicate effectively while on the other side of the world. Just remember it is often what is not said that is the real topic. I so often see couples argue about the strangest things, and my wife and I have had some of these occasions. It helps if I remind myself in the beginning that there is a deeper topic, a question she is asking without words. In most cases, that question is "Am I lovely? Am I loved? Am I worth fighting for?"* I write about this in my blog. I hope you can get some time to read it at http://www.TheAuthorOfMarriage.com.

Let's keep this discussion open. Feel free to use this as your pre-married counseling session.

To James:

I agree about the strange arguments. I have kept things to myself and reacted unfairly on other subjects later on. Also, sometimes I express myself on a concern that I feel is valid but I know is just caused by stress. Yet this still leads to a confrontation even if I explain that I know I was wrong for feeling that way, but I just wanted to talk to someone about it. I find myself almost always without someone who is likeminded or has a strong faith base to talk to. What should I do when I need feedback or another point of view but can't talk to my loved one because it will just start a conversation that is unnecessary or about something I'm not completely sure about?

To R:

It may be difficult to do all that I suggest where you are. But I often recommend that even after being married, as important as it is to have a date night with your spouse, it is also important to have a guys' night and a girls' night out occasionally. Cindy and I try to do this every week.

---

* Eldredge. *Wild at Heart.*

God never intended our spouses to meet all of our relationship needs; you have described a perfect example. That is why I have always loved the verse that speaks about iron sharpening iron. I believe it is speaking to the conversations we need to have with other men—we talk and clash swords, sometimes agreeing and sometimes not, and during the clashing we find our place; we either solidify our view or take up a new one. Many times men think that when they get married they will have all those conversations with their wives. But as you have alluded to, there are some topics that will cause them to worry; others will threaten their security. And as you also mentioned, there are some topics that you have not yet worked out and you are not even sure what you believe.

I am not saying that we keep secrets or are dishonest in any way, only that we seek other godly men to clash swords with and discuss topics that may not be helpful or uplifting for our wives to hear.

As far as bringing up things that need to be discussed, it is hard to say unless I know what the topic was. I do think sometimes that we talk too much and do not ask enough questions. The goal is to understand each other. You may not always agree, but you should still pursue understanding.

If you will share a few details, I think I can help you work through it so that if you experience it again, you will have the tools to communicate effectively about it.

I look forward to hearing back from you.

My friend "R" has asked some great questions. Just so you know, "R" is still in Iraq at the time of this writing, and I am pleased to say that he continues to seek godly counsel before his upcoming marriage after he returns to the States.

ARGUMENTS: BETH MOORE—AND MY CONFESSION

Now I'd like to show you a correspondence I had with a woman who's been married for twenty years. "D" visits my blog on marriage through my Facebook page, and I thought you'd enjoy her insights!

To James:

I love this woman's Bible Studies.

But she may as well have hit me over the head when I listened to Focus on the Family's "Focus on Marriage" DVD.* One of her points reminded me of one of your articles. We women want perfection. But her take on it was a bit harder on the women because she asked us, "Isn't 'good' good?"

We women spend much of our youth dreaming about a Prince Charming to protect, rescue, and romance us the rest of our lives. And we want our husband to be that Prince at all times.

When I'm in a bad mood, can't he understand that I just want a hug? ('Cause why wouldn't the prince want to hug a porcupine?) Why can't he see the things

---

* Focus on the Family. *Focus on Marriage* Simulcast Event on DVD.

that need to be done around the house without me telling him? Goodness, we've been married for twenty years! Does he still need instruction (the reason many women refer to their husbands as another child)?

The truth is that we women want even more than that because even when you do something nice for us, we often question your methods, intention, or skill. And, minutes after receiving this gift/action from you, if we find your underwear in front of the clothes hamper (inches from INSIDE the clothes hamper) all loving thoughts are erased.

That "buzz" of early love, which hides imperfection, wears off. It visits occasionally, but not often enough to hide his flaws (or mine) anymore.

Beth [Moore] was suggesting that perfect marriages don't exist. Perfect men don't exist. We all stumble— that's a fact. But do you have a "good" man? Do you have a "good" marriage, if not perfect? And she was pleading with young marrieds to stick it out—don't give up on your marriage just because it isn't everything you dreamed it would be. Because, isn't "good" good?

I'll be honest. I was both saddened and challenged by that. Frankly, I'd really like to be married to Prince Charming. I believe I have worked tirelessly to make my husband a close facsimile. (Don't think I don't recognize the irony of my imperfectness.) So, I'm a little frustrated by having to accept "good" when I want amazing.

My husband is a GOOD man. I'd never trade him for any man on this earth. My marriage is a GOOD marriage.

And, after 20 years, you'd think I'd have realized all this and stopped getting my feelings hurt when HE's not meeting all my varied needs. Only God can do that. —D.

To D:

WOW! Now I am going to have to put your name in the credits of my book. Please? Can I use this? I think maybe you should be writing your own book.

Thanks a million for sharing.

To James:

I'm just re-wording Beth [Moore]. Don't be afraid to crack the whip with us women. Our dripping faucets could use a bit of tightn'n!

To D:

Yeah, that is the one thing I am not called to do (point out the mistakes of wives), but by all means I can put something like this in the book and it will come across better because it is coming from a woman.

LOL—It is so much better for us to point out our own mistakes and laugh at ourselves than to be pointing out each other's and causing fights.

To James:

A foolish son is his father's ruin, and a quarrelsome wife is like a constant dripping (Prov. 19:13).

Before You Communicate, Agree that You Care

Good communication begins after you both agree that you care. I know this may seem rather obvious, but it is one of two necessary components of good communication.

It is easy to say, "Of course I care," but do each of you care more about the other than you do about yourself? This is the true definition of *love* as modeled by the sacrifice of Jesus' life on the cross for us.

Before you let that overwhelming definition of *love* discourage you, let me assure you that this is a lifelong process that begins with a commitment or decision. The important thing is to understand that good communication requires that you care.

The second thing required is that you have good communication skills. Everyone thinks they are better than they really are.

Good communication skills include lots of questions and lots of listening. It is extremely hard for most people to separate their need to be understood from their desire to understand the other person. It's absolutely necessary to identify whose issue is being discussed in each conversation.

Obviously, not every conversation has to be about an issue. But when either of you has an issue that needs to be discussed that does not seem to get resolved easily, then you can use the skills I will share with you, which are similar to those in Harville Hendrix's *Getting the Love You Want.* *

---

* Hendrix. *Getting the Love You Want.*

The first important communication skill is to agree whose issue is being discussed. Once you have agreed, you must agree that the person who has the issue is the one who has the floor. I have found that holding something like a cell phone helps as a physical sign that you have agreed together who needs to be understood. And that is the only goal of the person listening. Being a good listener means you will focus all your attention on understanding the other.

The person who has the issue will talk and explain the issue, including what happened or what was said, how he/she felt, and what he/she wants to do or wants his/her partner to do.

Once the talker is finished talking about the issue, that person can indicate he/she is finished. Then the listener should repeat back in his/her own words what he/she heard, making sure to identify feelings and desires of the other. When the listener is finished repeating what he/she heard, the listener should ask, "Did I understand you properly?" Usually the talker will say yes but may need to clarify or add something. This process can sometimes go back and forth several times. The speaker will not relinquish the talking item (cell phone) until he/she can say, "Yes, I think you completely understand me on this issue."

It is often very hard for the listener not to jump in and add things or bring up his/her own issues in the middle of this process. The listener needs to avoid this and pursue complete understanding of his/her partner. The listener needs to understand that he/she will get the same respect and focus when it is his/her turn.

Sometimes it is helpful to have someone coach you through this process and enforce some guidelines. This is what I often do as a relationship coach.

Having and using skills combined with caring for each other and putting each other first will lead to good communication.

Speaking of communicating, I hope you'll take the time to email my wife and me at james@theauthorofmarriage.com with your personal questions about marriage. We'd love to know how this book has touched your life or the life of a friend or family member. For more insights on living a godly marriage, please join my interactive blog at www.TheAuthorofMarriage.com.

BIBLIOGRAPHY

Chapman, Gary. *Covenant Marriage: Building Communication and Intimacy.* Nashville: B&H Publishing, 2003.

Chapman, Gary. *The Five Love Languages: How to Express Heartfelt Commitment to Your Mate.* Chicago: Northfield Publishing, 1995.

Eldredge, John. *Wild at Heart: Discovering the Secret of a Man's Soul.* Nashville: Thomas Nelson, Inc., 2001.

Focus on the Family. *Focus on Marriage* Simulcast Event on DVD. www.focusonthefamily.com.

Hendrix, Harville. *Getting the Love You Want: The Guide for Couples.* New York: Harper Perennial, 1988.

Hession, Roy. *The Calvary Road.* England: Roy Hession Book Trust, 1950. http://www.christianissues.biz/pdf-bin/sanctification/thecalvaryroad.pdf.

Meyer, Joyce. *Battlefield of the Mind: Winning the Battle in Your Mind.* New York: FaithWords, 2002.

Smalley, Gary and John Trent, PhD. *Love is a Decision.* New York: Pocket Books, 1993.

IF YOU'RE A FAN OF THIS BOOK, PLEASE TELL OTHERS...

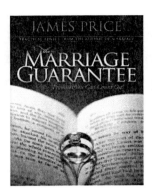

- Write about *The Marriage Guarantee* on your blog, Twitter, MySpace, or Facebook page.
- Suggest *The Marriage Guarantee* to friends.
- When you're in a bookstore, ask them if they carry the book. The book is available through all major distributors so any bookstore that does not have *The Marriage Guarantee* in stock can easily order it.
- Write a positive review of *The Marriage Guarantee* on www.amazon.com.
- Send my publisher, HigherLife Publishing, suggestions on websites, conferences, and events you know of where this book could be offered at info@ahigherlife.com.
- Purchase additional copies to give away as gifts.

CONNECT WITH ME...

To learn more about *The Marriage Guarantee—Promises You Can Count On!* and for insights on living a godly marriage, please join my interactive blog at www.TheAuthorofMarriage.com.

YOU MAY ALSO CONTACT MY PUBLISHER DIRECTLY:

HigherLife Development Services, Inc.
400 Fontana Circle
Building 1 – Suite 105
Oviedo, Florida 32765
Phone: (407) 563-4806
Email: info@ahigherlife.com

We live in an amazing day and age when products we buy almost alway come with a guarantee—that wonderful little paper that says that i the product doesn't work or we're not satisfied, the manufacturer wil exchange it or give us our money back! From appliances to cars to toys to clothes.. did you know that even *your marriage* has a guarantee?

The guarantee comes from God, who is the author of marriage. The guarantee is seer in I Corinthians 13:8 where He says…

LOVE NEVER FAILS.

If we learn to love like God wants us to, then WE WILL NOT FAIL.

The Marriage Guarantee walks you through the guarantees God has for you marriage. The foundations of the Guarantees include:

- Forgiveness
- Faith
- Resolving conflict
- Communication
- Service

If you feel like your marriage should be on a recall list or is not living up to the manufacturer's promise, then *The Marriage Guarantee* is just what you've been waiting for.

JAMES PRICE developed a vision for family ministry as a young child growing up in Venezuela where his parents served with New Tribes Mission. He has since served couples and families for over 15 years and currently serves at Northland, A Church Distributed, teaching classes on marriage as well as coaching and pastoral counseling of pre-married and married couples. He has been married to his wife, Cindy, for 16 years and currently resides in Longwood, FL, with his wife and two children, Matthew and Heather.

RELIGION
Christian Life / Love & Marriage

$14.99
ISBN 978-1-935245-21-6
51499>
9 781935 245216

HIGHERLIFE
PUBLISHING
www.ahigherlife.com